Merchandise
Planning
WORKBOOK

fb

Merchandise Planning *WORKBOOK*

ROSETTA S. LAFLEUR
UNIVERSITY OF DELAWARE

FAIRCHILD BOOKS
NEW YORK

*To my family, both near and in spirit, who anchors me
in love and support*

Vice President & General Manager, Fairchild Education & Conference Division: Elizabeth Tighe
Executive Editor: Olga T. Kontzias
Senior Associate Acquiring Editor: Jaclyn Bergeron
Assistant Acquisitions Editor: Amanda Breccia
Editorial Development Director: Jennifer Crane
Development Editor: Sylvia L. Weber
Associate Art Director: Erin Fitzsimmons
Production Director: Ginger Hillman
Production Editor: Jessica Rozler
Project Manager: Jeff Hoffman
Copyeditor: Rayhane Sanders
Ancillaries Editor: Noah Schwartzberg
Cover Design: Erin Fitzsimmons
Cover Art: iStockPhoto
Text Design: Mike Suh/Tronvig Kuypers
Page Composition: Precision Graphics
Director, Sales & Marketing: Brian Normoyle

Library of Congress Catalog Card Number: 2008940706

ISBN 978-1-56367-749-6

GST R 133004424

Printed in the United States of America

TP13

Contents

Extended Contents

Chapter 2   **Excel Formulas**   *21*

Chapter 3   **Planning**   *31*

Chapter 4 **Sales Planning** *49*

Chapter 5 **Inventory** *73*

Chapter 6 **Planning Reductions** *95*

Chapter 7 **Planning Purchases** 115

Preface

Students who complete curricula in fashion or retail merchandising are expected to have a thorough understanding of retail mathematics and to be proficient in developing merchandise plans and using computer applications. This workbook was written to help them meet those expectations, specifically in courses in merchandising math and merchandise planning. Microsoft Excel is the most commonly used nonproprietary application in the fashion industry for planning. But in retail companies that use proprietary planning systems such as Arthur, Retail Pro, or Martec, employees are expected to be knowledgeable of the planning process and retail mathematics in order to interpret data generated by these planning systems. An important feature of this text is that it addresses multiple skills and competency development in the areas of retail math, Excel computer applications, merchandise planning, and the retail method of inventory valuation. This workbook is organized around understanding mathematics related to five progressive planning concepts: sales, inventory, reductions, purchases, and margins. The emphasis is on understanding the *what*, *why*, *how*, *how to*, and *what ifs* of merchandise planning concepts. For example:

► *What* should be planned (sales, inventory, reductions, purchases, etc.)?

► *Why* (the sequence of planning and the relationships among planning concepts)

- *How* sales, inventory, reductions, purchases, and margins generate profit; *how* the computer can be used as a tool to aid understanding of retail mathematics

- *How to* use Excel as a tool to develop merchandise plans by structuring retail formulas to quickly calculate sales, inventory, reductions, purchases, margins, cost values, and profit values

- *What if* planned variables are increased or decreased (how are formula results affected, and what is the resulting impact on profit)?

Excel computer application exercises are the major component of this book and require students to develop two separate Excel files. One file is used to complete over fifty computer applications as they are worked through the chapters. In these exercises, standard formulas used in the retail trade are outlined and highlighted in step-by-step applications designed to illustrate formulas and increase proficiency in retail math and Excel. The emphasis in the applications exercises is on developing and applying correct formats to worksheets and structuring retail formulas by using cell references to make formulas interactive. Interactive formulas allow students to see and understand the *what ifs* of planning. For example, the impact of an increase or decrease in a markdown percent on an initial markup (IMU) can be easily understood by changing cell values and observing the recalculated IMU value. Some retail formulas, such as the percentage variation method of planning inventory, are complex and may be difficult for some students to understand. Because computer exercises require components of formulas to be calculated in sequential steps, formulas can be dissected to show which cells are involved in the calculations and what values are being computed. Afterwards, Excel skill development is stressed through combining the calculation steps and structuring single complex formulas.

The second file is used exclusively to complete seven sequential merchandise planning assignments. At the end of Chapters Four–Ten, assignments require students to use a previously developed planning form and apply concepts and formulas from each chapter. For example, a sales plan for a six-month period is the assignment for Chapter Four. When Chapter Five is completed, the assignment requires students to make a copy of the previously calculated sales plan and develop an inventory plan based on the planned sales values. Each plan is completed on a separate worksheet and the same Excel file is used for all assignments throughout the workbook. Completing assignments in one file with multiple worksheets allows students to review each step separately and to see the unified, sequential relationships among planning concepts.

The workbook is divided into ten chapters. Chapter One offers an introduction to Excel's new Microsoft Office Fluent user interface. A review of basic Excel features is introduced. Two computer exercises are included at the end of Chapter One that require students to use Excel to design, format, and print a six-month planning form that will be used to complete the seven chapter assignments. Even though an introduction to Excel 2007 is the focus of Chapter One, all the computer exercises in this book can be completed using the basic spreadsheet functions and features available in earlier versions of Excel.

Chapter Two focuses on formulas and formula auditing. The use of absolute and relative cell references and the order of mathematical operations are emphasized as ways to efficiently structure simple and complex retail formulas covered in application exercises. Chapter Three covers the importance of planning, planning levels, types of merchandise plans, and organizational structures that support merchandise-planning activities, as well as the importance of planning in accomplishing profit objectives.

The basics of developing a merchandise dollar plan in sequential steps are covered in Chapters Four–Eight. A six-month planning form is used as a framework for understanding planning concepts related to sales, inventory, reductions, purchases, margins, and profit. In each chapter, learning objectives and key terms are provided along with minimal, but relevant, amounts of background information related to planning concepts. The objective is not to lose students in detailed narratives but to provide a background for the planning sequence, retail math, application exercises, and formulas that will be covered as they work through the chapters. This approach allows the workbook either to stand alone or to serve as a supplement to other texts and readings for more in-depth discussions of concepts. Computer applications show methods of planning inventory, calculating sell through, OTB (open-to-buy), and IMU—all of which allow for comparisons and analyses of calculated values.

Chapter Nine addresses the retail method of inventory valuation for the purpose of understanding calculations of cost values. The six-month planning form includes a section devoted to planning cost values so connections between cost, retail, and profit can be highlighted.

Gross margin (GM), gross-margin returns on inventory investments (GMROI), and profit and loss are covered in Chapter Ten. Students use formulas to reference values required to calculate GMs and operating profits from their completed planning form and develop six monthly gross-margin reports. The interactive nature of the spreadsheet allows the planned variables to be adjusted, resulting in recalculation of all referenced cells in the budget plan and GM reports. The resulting impacts on all planned variables and profit can thus be understood and analyzed. After the plan and GM reports are completed, the professor can instruct students to adjust the budget by changing cell values to achieve specific planning objectives, such as an even distribution of sales, an even distribution of receipts, or an improvement of the GMROI.

Features of this workbook include the following:

▶ It presents concepts in progressive steps.

▶ Only two assignment files are used throughout the workbook.

▶ Each assignment builds on previous assignments.

▶ Retail formulas are presented in narrative format.

▶ Alternate methods of developing formulas are presented.

▶ Examples include spreadsheet screenshots with accompanying formulas.

▶ Multiple application exercises promote hands-on learning.

▶ Formula structures are illustrated and explained.

By taking advantage of these features, students can transfer the skills they have mastered in school to the retail workplace and can begin their careers with experience and competence.

Acknowledgments

If you count all your assets, you always show a profit ~Robert Quillen

I wish to acknowledge as my assets all those who contributed to the inception, development, and completion of this book.

I am especially indebted to my FASH 418 students of the University of Delaware. Their enthusiasm, interests, and quest for knowledge provided me with the inspiration and impetus to embark on this endeavor and bring it to fruition.

Sincere thanks to the staff of Fairchild Publications. Thank you Olga Kontzias for encouraging me to develop a course packet into a published book. To my editor Sylvia Weber, thank you for your calm and assuring manner in guiding me through the development phase of this project. I am grateful for your continuous encouragement, ideas, and suggestions in shaping the content and organization of this book. To Erin Fitzsimmons, Jessica Rozler, and Jeff Hoffman thank you for your assistance in managing all the technical complexities required to bring this book to production.

Special appreciation is extended to individuals in the retail industry for their ideas and contributions: Brian Deleu, J.C. Penney; Lisa Holder, Jos. A. Bank; Steven Siegler, J. McLaughlin; Craig Snyderman, Kohls; and Donna Hardcastle, Macy Corp.

To Jeanne M. Horton, Katherine Conway-Turner, Sandra Hines, Charlene Benson, Araya Debassay, Peter Carmen, and Judy VanName thank you for your friendship, counsel, and moral support during the completion of this project.

To Francis Kwansa, I extend special acknowledgement for providing me with inspiration and encouragement. Your professional and personal contributions were invaluable in helping me to step out on this path and to move forward.

To my sister, Delores S. Galloway, my niece Denise S. Washington, and her husband James, thank you for being there for me and providing me with an ambulance of your time, support, and comfort.

1 *Introduction to Excel 2007*

Chapter Objectives

After reading this chapter you should be able to:

- ▶ Open the Excel application.
- ▶ Explain how Excel 2007 differs from previous versions.
- ▶ Define *user interface*.
- ▶ Use correct terminology to identify parts of the Excel 2007 window.
- ▶ Compare tools in the Excel window for performing different design and formatting tasks.
- ▶ Explain the difference between a workbook and a worksheet.
- ▶ Distinguish between structural components of a worksheet.
- ▶ Explain and describe ways to modify a worksheet's structure.
- ▶ Use specifications to design and format a worksheet.
- ▶ Explain and describe ways to set up a worksheet for printing.
- ▶ Apply page setup specifications and print a worksheet.

Proficiency in developing and using spreadsheets is a technical skill required of professionals in the fashion industry. The importance of this skill for those preparing for careers in the fashion retail sector cannot be overemphasized. Spreadsheets deliver fast calculations for reporting and analyzing data from a variety of sources. As a tool for performing mathematical calculations, spreadsheets allow data to be easily organized in ways that are flexible for repetitive computations and quick changes. This chapter provides an overview of spreadsheets; however, a basic familiarity with computers and spreadsheets is assumed.

NEW FEATURES IN EXCEL 2007

Excel 2007 is the latest release in the Microsoft Office suite. While the new version of the spreadsheet application retains capabilities of earlier releases, Excel 2007 features a new **user interface (UI)** to make working with worksheets easier and more efficient. *User interface* refers to the way commands, tools, and features are visually arranged in the window (Figure 1.1). Excel 2007's document window looks very different from previous versions that you may have used. While all the functions of the previous versions still exist in Excel 2007, there are important new features and refinements to the application.

Ribbon
Instead of the traditional menu and toolbar, the window has a new feature called the **ribbon**. The ribbon is made up of eight standard tabs including **Home**, **Insert**, **Page Layout**, **Formula**, **Data**, **Preview**, and **View**. Commands are grouped on task-oriented tabs and organized by activities required to complete tasks. For example, the home tab is made up of groups including **Clipboard**, **Font**, **Alignment**, **Number**, **Styles**, **Cells**, and **Editing** (Figure 1.2).

Contextual Tabs
Contextual tabs that are relevant to some applications appear on the ribbon only when specific tasks are being performed. For example, as shown in Figure 1.1, a contextual Table tab is on the ribbon and provides additional design and formatting tools. Similar tabs exist for charts, pictures, and objects.

Quick Access Toolbar
A quick access toolbar, located in the upper left corner, above the ribbon, provides access to commands used most often. A drop-down list on the tool-

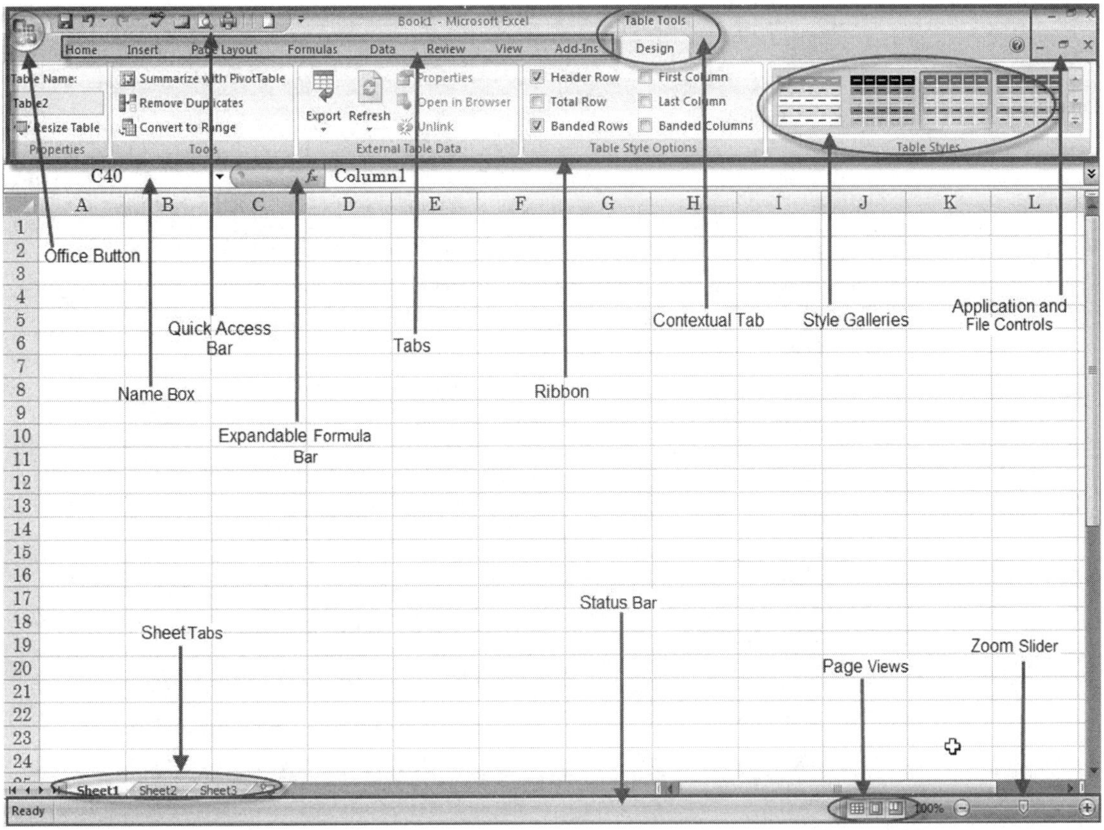

Figure 1.1 Excel 2007 user interface

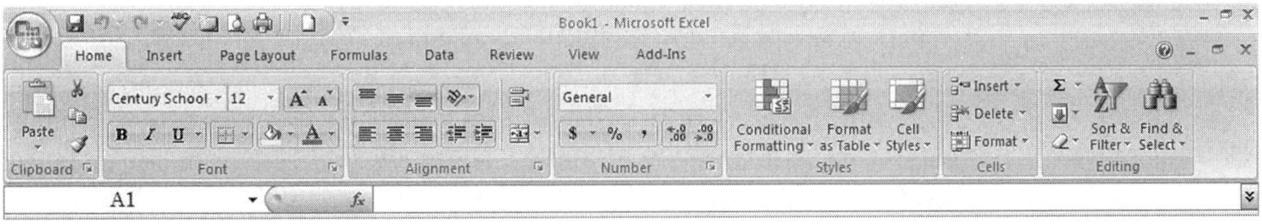

Figure 1.2 Excel ribbon

bar has selections for customizing and relocating the quick access toolbar above or below the ribbon (Figure 1.1).

Microsoft Office Button

The office button, located in the upper left of the ribbon, has commands that previously appeared on the file menu. The office button provides a list of the

Figure 1.3 Office
button commands

50 most recently used files. Regularly used files can be *pin-tacked* in the list for easy access (Figure 1.3).

Other options in the Office button allow customization of document features as well as access to online templates and resources for updating Excel.

Additions to Status Bar

The status bar has 22 customizable worksheet features. A new **page layout** option allows the user to view how a document will look when it is printed, including margins, headers, and footers. Adjustments can be made to the worksheet in the page layout view to achieve the desired printout. A zoom slider has been added to the status bar to provide easy magnification ranging from 10 percent to 500 percent (Figure 1.1).

Themes and Style Galleries

Document themes are built-in page layout options consisting of formatting choices designed to give documents a professional appearance. Themes include sets of predefined coordinated colors, fonts, lines, fill patterns, and effects that are applied to an entire document. Style galleries are predefined, theme-based formatting options for cell content, including formats for data, alignment, titles, and numbers (Figure 1.4).

Live Preview

Live preview shows how formats and styles will look on a worksheet. When the mouse moves over a style gallery, format and style effects are shown on a worksheet before they are applied.

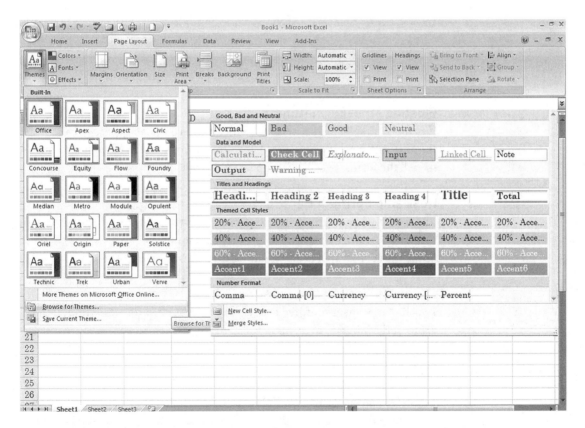

Figure 1.4 Document themes and cell styles menus

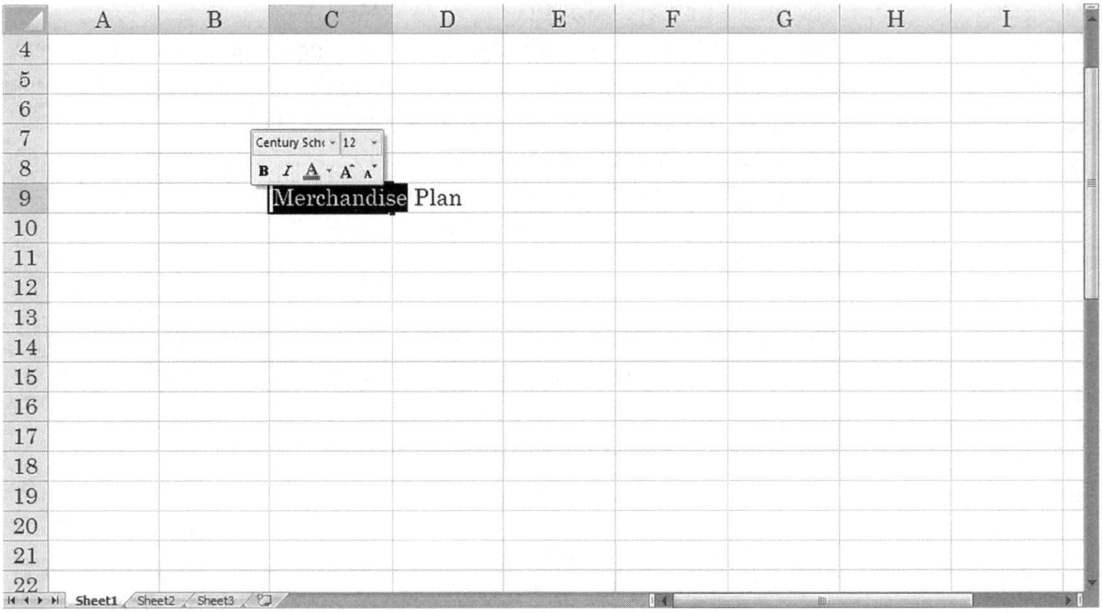

Figure 1.5 Floating mini-formatting bar

Floating Mini–Formatting Bar

When text is selected on a worksheet, a formatting bar appears directly over the text and provides standard text-formatting tools. When text is deselected, the formatting bar disappears (Figure 1.5).

Resizable Formula Bar

The formula bar can be resized to accommodate long formulas and extensive text. In addition, there is an **auto complete menu** feature to assist in developing the correct syntax and arguments for formulas (Figure 1.6).

Enhanced Sorting and Filtering

Data that meet user-defined criteria can be custom sorted and filtered by cell value, cell color, cell icon, and font color.

New File Formats

All Excel 2007 documents are saved with in an .xlxs file extension, which is an extensive markup language (XML)-based file format. XML format allows data to be moved easily among different Microsoft Office applications including Word and PowerPoint. Note that while workbooks created in Excel 2007 can

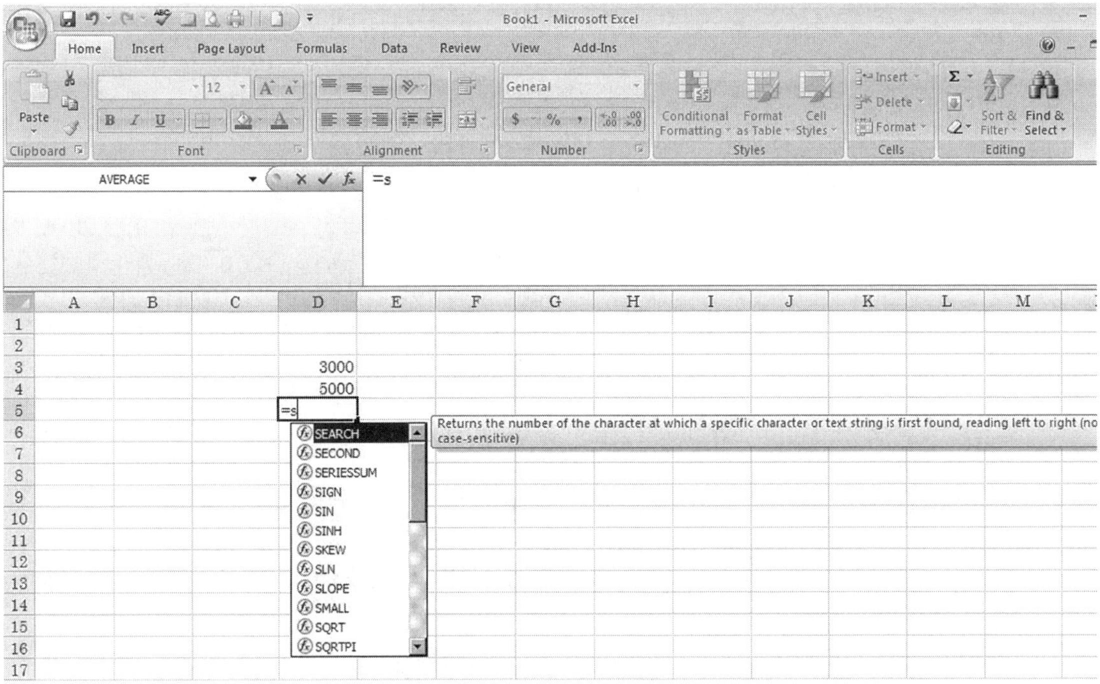

Figure 1.6 Expandable formula bar and auto complete formula menu

be saved in earlier versions of Excel, some of the newer formatting features may be lost. Excel 2007 has a compatibility checker which lists compatibility problems that may arise if a workbook is saved in a format other than XML. A file converter is required to open an Excel 2007 workbook in earlier versions of Excel.

Application Exercise 1.1 Explore the Excel User Interface

If your Excel application is located on the desktop, you can double-click on the icon to open Excel. Otherwise, start the Excel application by selecting **Start** on your desktop to display the start menu. Then select: **Programs> Microsoft Office> Microsoft Office Excel 2007**. You will notice that when the application opens, a new workbook entitled **Book 1** opens in the window.

1. To examine selections on the ribbon, Click on the drop-down menu next to the **Quick Access Bar.** Select *Show below the Ribbon* and notice that the access bar is relocated. Select *Minimize the Ribbon* from the

drop-down menu and notice that the ribbon is reduced to show only the office button, tabs, and quick access bar. To maximize the ribbon, select *Minimize the Ribbon* again to cancel the selection.

2. Select the **Home Tab** which is the first tab on the ribbon.

   - Notice that the home tab has seven groups with tools for specific tasks. As you move your cursor over the tools, Tool Tips appear to tell you what they are for.
   - Notice that the **Clipboard**, **Font**, **Alignment**, and **Number** groups all have a small arrow located in the lower right corners. This indicates that expanded menus are associated with the groups.
   - Click on the arrow associated with the font group to see that the expanded menu is the dialogue box that was available in previous versions of Excel.

3. Type a phrase in any cell on the worksheet to see the floating **Mini–Formatting Bar**. Double-click in the cell to edit the phrase and notice that the mini-formatting bar appears. Make selections from the bar to format the text.

4. Expand and resize the **Formula Bar** by clicking and dragging the bottom edge.

5. Examine the **Status Bar**:

   - Increase and decrease the magnification of the worksheet by moving the **Zoom Slider**.
   - Click on **Page Layout** view to see how the worksheet will look when printed. Notice that rows and columns are visible and that there are placeholders for headers and footers.
   - **Right-click** on the **Status Bar** to see the menu of customized options.

6. Examine the **Office Button**:

   - Select *Excel Options* to see how Excel documents can be customized. Click on each Excel option listed in the left pane and notice that a description of the custom feature appears in the right pane. Click *OK* to close.
   - Examine *Save As* by **highlighting** it from the Office button menu. Notice the different save options. Select *Save As* an **Excel Workbook.** Name the workbook *Examination of Ribbon* and save it to your desktop. Close the file.

   Note: Because this file was created to acquaint you with features of Excel 2007 and will not be used for any other application exercises or assignments, you may delete it from your desktop.

THE EXCEL 2007 WORKSHEET

An Excel file is referred to as a *workbook*. Like a textbook, a workbook has multiple pages or *worksheets*. The number of sheets in a workbook is limited only by the computer's memory. When the Excel application is first opened, a blank workbook named *Book 1* is created. By default, a workbook contains three worksheets. A worksheet is best described as a computerized ledger that allows you to create, organize, analyze, and manage data. All worksheets have the same basic components that can be customized with templates and other selections from the ribbon.

Structural Components of Worksheets

A worksheet is composed of a grid formed by rows and columns. An Excel 2007 worksheet comprises over one million rows and approximately 16,000 columns. At the intersection of numerically labeled rows and alphabetized columns are cells. Data, in the form of values and labels, is entered in cells. Each cell is identified by a unique reference designated by its corresponding row and column. In cells containing numerical data, formulas and functions are used to perform mathematical calculations and statistical analysis. Cells with data can be easily added or deleted, sorted, rearranged, and formatted for effective analysis and reporting.

All worksheets contain the following seven common structural components (Figure 1.7):

▶   A **cell** is the intersection of a row and column.

▶   A **row** is formed by cells aligned horizontally.

▶   A **column** is formed by cells aligned vertically.

▶   A **cell address** or *cell reference* is the corresponding row and column that form a cell.

▶   A **cell range** is a group of cells defined by the number of rows and columns, e.g. 2R x 2C.

▶   A **value** is a number or data.

▶   A **label** is text that describes or identifies the cell's content.

Modifying Worksheet Structure

The default design of a worksheet is multiple cells identical in size and shape. To be effective, worksheets must be designed in ways to make them easy to use. This requires modifications to specify the number and size of rows and columns, which cells will hold information, how the information will be identified

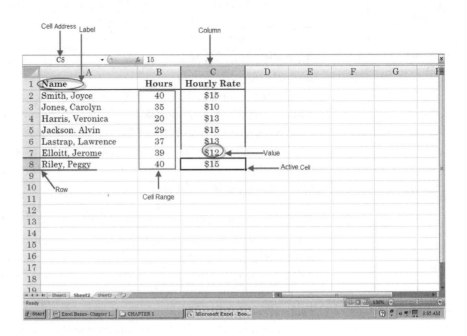

Figure 1.7
Structural
components of a
worksheet

in cells, and the formulas and formats required in cells to produce the desired results. Good worksheet design makes it easy to enter, organize, and manipulate data and minimizes errors in interpreting and analyzing information.

Moving Around in a Worksheet

Common worksheet terminology that relates to navigating and modifying worksheets includes the following:

▶ **Select**. To select a cell or cell range, hold down the left mouse button and move over the area you wish to select on the worksheet. When the mouse button is released, the selected area becomes the active cell or range. When the cursor is moved over the black border of a selected area, it becomes a double-cross arrow. The left mouse button must be pressed and held to use the arrow to move cells and ranges. When the Ctrl key is held and the cursor is moved over the black border of a selected area, a double "+" becomes attached to the cursor. The cursor must be pressed and held to duplicate cells and ranges to other areas of a worksheet.

▶ **Fill handle**. Once a cell is selected, it is outlined in a bold black border. The small square in the lower right of the active cell is the fill handle. The fill handle must be pressed, held, and moved over adjacent cells to fill with the content of the active cell.

- **Right-click**. This term refers to pressing the right mouse button when a worksheet area is selected. When pressed, menu options related to the area appear on the worksheet.

- **Drag and drop**. This term refers to selecting a cell or range and holding down the left mouse button as the content is moved, or dragged, to another area. *Drop* refers to releasing the left mouse button to deposit the content to the area.

There are several ways to navigate among cells on a worksheet. On small worksheets, the simplest way is to use the mouse to select the cell. On large worksheets it may be easier to use shortcut keys, the scroll bar, a combination of the Ctrl key and arrow keys, or the *Find and Go To* commands. Multiple noncontiguous cells, rows, or columns can be selected for formatting by holding down the Ctrl key as selections are made.

Adjusting Worksheet Rows and Columns

The default width for Excel columns is 8.43 characters wide. The default size for Excel rows is 15 points high. Column width can be increased to a maximum of 255 characters and row height to a maximum of 409 points. There are four ways to increase the height and width of rows and columns, including:

- Select the row or column and drag it to the desired size.

- Select *Format* from the cells group on the home tab and select *Auto Fit* for the row height or column width.

- Right-click on a row or column, select height or width, then type in the desired size value.

- Double-click on the border of the column or row to expand to fit the widest or highest content.

Adding, Deleting, or Merging Worksheet Cells, Rows, and Columns

The cells group on the home tab has **Insert** and **Delete** commands for cells, rows, columns, and sheets. The same commands are available when the cell, row, or column is right-clicked.

When a cell or cell range is added or deleted, there is an option to shift cells left, right, up, or down. When a row is added, it is inserted above the active row. When a column is added, it is inserted to the left of the active column.

Merge converts a group of cells into a single cell. Cells are merged for the purpose of worksheet design or to improve the presentation of worksheet data. On the home tab, the tool to merge and center data that extends over multiple cells into one cell is located in the alignment group. When cells containing multiple data are merged, only the uppermost data is retained. Merged cells retain the cell address of the upper left cell in the group. Once merged, cell contents cannot be moved to a single cell without first unmerging. To unmerge, highlight the cell and click on the merge and center tool in the alignment group.

An alternative to merging cells is **Wrap Text**. This feature will make the contents of a cell visible by expanding the row and displaying contents in multiple lines. The row will expand in depth to accommodate the number of lines in the cell.

Entering and Editing Worksheet Content

When labels are typed in a cell, the default alignment is left. For values, the default alignment is right. The **Editing** group on the home tab has tools for selecting, finding, and replacing information in a worksheet. Data, including values and labels, can be entered and edited on a worksheet by typing directly into cells or the formula bar. A custom list is an option available through the **Office Button** or **Excel Options.** In addition to the built-in custom list of months and days, users can set up custom lists of regularly used text. Once established, the fill handle can be used to fill selected cells with the items from a custom list.

Moving and Duplicating Worksheet Areas

When duplicate data are required on different parts of a worksheet, they can be copied by using tools from the **Clipboard** group. Another way of copying is dragging and dropping cell content to another location while holding the Ctrl key. This feature can also be used to duplicate contents of entire rows or columns. In this case, the row or column heading must first be selected to move or duplicate contents.

Renaming and Copying a Worksheet

The default name for a worksheet is **Sheet**. When there are multiple worksheets in a workbook, sheets can be renamed and moved to rearrange. The sheet menu can be accessed by a right click on the **sheet tab** at the bottom of the worksheet. In addition to relocating a worksheet, choices are available to copy, add, delete, hide, and protect a worksheet. In addition, sheet tabs can be colored to make sheets easier to identify in a workbook.

Formatting a Worksheet

Cells can be formatted before data are entered into them. Excel 2007 has a gallery of predefined styles for cells. Other formats for values and labels can be developed by making formatting selections from either the **Font,**

Alignment, or **Number** groups on the home tab. Once a format is applied to one part of a worksheet, the **Format Painter** can be used to quickly copy it to other parts of a worksheet. Select the cell containing the format to be copied. Next, select the **Format Painter** icon from the clipboard group and then select the cells to be formatted. The format will be applied to the cells.

Application Exercise 1.2 **Design and Format an Excel Worksheet**

In this application you will design and format the Excel worksheet that you will use to complete all chapter assignments in this workbook.

1. Start your Excel application by selecting **Start** to display the start menu. Then select: **Programs>Microsoft Office>Microsoft Office Excel 2007**.

2. When **Book 1** opens, immediately save it as an Excel file by selecting from the Office Button menu: **Save As>Excel Workbook**.

    Rename the file *[your last name] Merchandise Budget*. Save this file to your USB drive or desktop. Now you are ready to begin designing your worksheet.

3. Figure 1.8 is an example of the worksheet that you will develop. Use Tables 1.1 and 1.2, containing specifications for rows, columns, labels, and value formats.

    Most of the tools that you will use are located on the home tab and page layout tabs.

    Notice that the worksheet is divided into three sections: *season, retail values, and cost values.*

4. Type the data labels in the same rows and columns as shown in Figure 1.8. Locations of the format tools and commands are provided in Tables 1.1 and 1.2. To help you locate them, they have been outlined with black boxes on the ribbon. Work in the normal view and save your file periodically by pressing the *save* icon on the **Quick Access Toolbar**.

5. When you finish, check to see that all your rows and columns are labeled the same as shown in Figure 1.8.

6. Check the format for the values by typing in a few numbers in rows labeled with dollar and percent signs. Afterwards, remove the numbers.

7. Run a spell-check on the worksheet.

8. Rename the sheet *Sales Plan*.

9. Save your file and exit Excel.

	A	B	C	D	E	F	G	H	I
1			SIX-MONTH MERCHANDISE BUDGET FOR A BASIC PRODUCT						
2				*Spring* ____					
3		**Planned**	**%**	**LY**					
4		Sales Increase/Decrease							
5		IMU (Initial Markup)							
6		Markdowns							
7		Sales Discounts							
8		Shrinkage							
9	Season	Operating Expenses							
10		Operating Profit							
11		Alterations /Workroom Expense							
12		Earned Cash Discounts							
13		Stock Turnover #							
14		Freight							
15		Maintained Markup Projection							
16		GMROI $							
17			Season/Total	FEB	MAR	APR	MAY	JUN	JUL
18		Sales $							
19		Sales %							
20									
21		BOM $							
22		Stock/Sales Ratio #							
23		EOM $							
24									
25		Markdown $							
26		Markdown % of Sales							
27		Markdown Distribution %							
28									
29		Sales Discounts $							
30		Discount % of Sales							
31	Retail Values	Discount Distribution %							
32									
33		Shrinkage $							
34		Shrinkage % of Sales							
35		Shrinkage Distribution %							
36									
37		Purchase@ Retail $							
38									
39		Cumulative Markup %							
40									
41		Average Inventory $							
42									
43		Stock Turnover #							
44									
45		Total Goods Handled @ Retail $							
46									
47		Gross Margin $							
48		Gross Margin %							
49									
50			Season/Total	FEB	MAR	APR	MAY	JUN	JUL
51		Purchase@ Cost $							
52									
53		Freight Cost $							
54									
55	Cost Values	BOM Cost $							
56									
57		EOM Cost $							
58									
59		Total Goods Handled @ Cost $							
60									
61		Cost of Goods Sold $							

Figure 1.8 Example of worksheet design

Table 1.1 Worksheet Design Specifications

Rows/Columns	Worksheet Design and Text Formats	Commands/Tools Locations
All Rows	Height = 18	Home Tab/Cells Group/Format
Column A	Width = 4	
Column B	Width = 35	
Columns C–I	Width = 17	
Entire Worksheet Font Face	Arial	Home Tab/Alignment Group /Font Group *Use Custom List feature to insert name of months in cells (D17:I17) and (D50:I50).*
Column A, Rows 3–16	Merge & Center/Rotate Text Up/Middle Align/ Bold Font/Size =16/Color Fill = Light Grey	
Column A, Rows 17–49	Merge & Center/Rotate Text Up/Middle Align/ Bold Font/Size = 16/Color Fill = Light Grey	
Column A, Rows 50–61	Merge & Center/Rotate Text Up/Middle Align/ Bold Font/Size = 16/Color Fill = Light Grey	
Column B, Rows 4–61	Left Align Text/Middle Align/Bold Font/Size = 14	
Row 1, Columns A–I	Merge & Center/Upper Case Font/Bold Font/ Size = 14	
Row 2, Columns A–I	Merge & Center/Italics Font/Bold Font/Size = 14	
Cells B3:D3	Color Fill = Light Grey/Center Text/Middle Align/Bold Font/Size = 14	
Cells B17:I17	Color Fill = Light Grey/Center Text/Middle Align/Bold Font/Size = 14 *Note: Font size for cell C17 must be 13 for label to fit in cell.*	
Cells B50:I50	Color Fill = Light Grey/Center Text/Middle Align/Bold Font/Size = 14 *Note: Font size for cell C55 must be 13 for label to fit in cell.*	
Cell C22	Color Fill = Light Grey	

Table 1.2   Format Specifications

Rows/Columns		Commands/Tools Locations
Cells C4:C12, C14:C15	Percentage/Decimal Places = 1/Center/ Middle Align/Bold Font/Size = 14	Home Tab/Number Group
Cell C13	Number/Decimal Places = 1/Negative Number (Red)/Center/ Middle Align/ Bold Font/Size = 14	Use Ctrl key to select multiple cells for formatting.
Cells C16, D4	Currency/Decimal Places = 0/Negative Number (Red)/Center/ Middle Align/ Bold Font/Size = 14	*Open expanded format options for numbers.* See the arrow pointing to expansion tool.
Cells C43:I43, D22:I22	Use Format Painter and paint *percent* format of Cell C13 to these cells.	
Column C–I, Rows 19, 26, 27, 30, 31, 34 35, 39, 48	Use Format Painter and paint *percent* format of Cell C4 to these rows.	
Column C–I, Rows 22, 43	Use Format Painter and paint *number* format of Cell C13 to these rows.	Home Tab/Clipboard Group
Columns C–I Rows 18, 21, 23, 25, 29, 33, 37, 41, 45, 47, 51, 53, 55, 57, 59, 61	Use Format Painter and paint *currency* format of Cell C16 to these rows.	
In cell D4	Use Format Painter and paint *currency* format of Cell C16 to this cell.	

PRINTING A WORKSHEET

Once design and format selections are completed, a worksheet can be set up for printing before entering data. A worksheet formatted and set up for printing can be saved as a **template**. Print setup involves determining the print area, page margins, paper size, and sheet orientation, and applying identifying worksheet information in headers and footers. All the tools required for print setup can be found in the **Page Setup** group on the **Page Layout** tab. The **Print Area** command has a tool for setting the area of the worksheet to be printed. When the desired area is highlighted and the **Set Print** tool is selected, the area is outlined by a broken line on the worksheet. When viewed in the page break preview, the area is outlined in a heavy blue line that can be adjusted. There are other options for adding to a selected print area and clearing the area.

A variety of paper sizes is offered with the option to orient as *portrait* or *landscape*. Predefined margins are available in the **Page Setup** group. The **Custom Margins** option opens expanded selections for setting left, right, top, bottom, and centering on a page. Header and footer margins can also be set through expanded selections. Headers and footers are areas on a worksheet in which identifying information about the worksheet can be inserted. When the **Page Layout** view is selected in the Status bar, an option to add a header or footer is presented. When selected, a contextual tab for designing the header or footer appears on the ribbon with preset selections for time, date, sheet name, file name and path, and page number. These text options can be positioned in the left, right, and center of the header or footer areas. Selections for aligning the header or footer with the margin and scaling with the worksheet's printed size are presented. Additional print setup features can be found in the **Scale to Fit** and **Sheet Options** groups. A print area can be printed at 100 percent of its original size or scaled to fit a percentage above or below the normal size. Scaling above or below the normal size affects the margins and the number of sheets required to print a worksheet. To print the gridlines and the header or footer on a worksheet, the selections must be selected from the Sheet Options groups.

Application Exercise 1.3 **Set Up and Print a Worksheet**

In this exercise you will develop the page setup and print specifications that you will use to print *each* worksheet that you complete as you work through the chapter assignments in this workbook. You will only have to complete the page setup once so that all your worksheets will print the same.

1. Start your Excel application by selecting **Start** on your desktop to display the start menu. Then select: **Programs > Microsoft Office > Microsoft Office Excel 2007**. Next, click on the **Office Button** located on the Ribbon and select **Open**. Once in the Open window, look on your desktop or in your USB drive and select your *Merchandise Budget* file worksheet that you designed and formatted in Application Exercise 1.2.

2. Table 1.3 contains the page setup specifications and provides locations of the page setup tools and commands. To help you locate them, they have been outlined with black boxes on the ribbon.

Table 1.3 Worksheet Print Setup Specifications

Setup Selections	Specifications	Commands/Tools Locations
Print Area	Begin at cell A1 and select 66 rows and 9 columns. Notice that in the last cell of your selection the cell range contained in the print area is displayed as: 61R x 9C Select *"Set Print Area"* after highlighting range.	
Orientation and Paper Size	Select "Letter" as paper size and "Portrait" orientation.	*Open expanded format options for page layout.* See arrow pointing to expansion tool.
Scaling	Adjust to 60% of normal size. *Because you will print on letter size paper, the scale of your worksheet needs to be reduced to fit on one page. Scale will not change the print area you selected.*	Click the *"Page"* tab.
Margins	From the expanded page setup box, select the *margins tab* and apply the following settings: Top = .75 Bottom = .25 Left = 0 Right = 0 Header = .50 Footer = .50 Center on Page = Horizontally Select *"OK."*	Click the *"Margins"* tab.
Header and Footer	Apply *Custom Header* as follows: Left section–type your name. Center section–select "Insert Date" button. Right section–select "Insert Time" button. Select *"OK."* In the sheet options group check: *"Scale with Document."* Apply *Custom Footer* as follows: Center section–select "Insert Sheet Name" button and press Enter key. Select "Insert File Name" button. Select *"OK"* twice to close expansion tool.	Click the *"Header/Footer"* tab.
Sheet Options	For gridlines, check: "Print" *Note: Even though sheet options allow the gridlines and column/row headings to be hidden in the worksheet window, they can still be included in a printout. If borders are applied to a worksheet they will be printed.*	Click the *"Sheet"* tab.

SIX-MONTH MERCHANDISE BUDGET FOR A BASIC PRODUCT

Spring _____

	Planned	%	LY					
Season	Sales Increase/Decrease							
	IMU (Initial Markup)							
	Markdowns							
	Sales Discounts							
	Shrinkage							
	Operating Expenses							
	Operating Profit							
	Alterations /Workroom Expense							
	Earned Cash Discounts							
	Stock Turnover #							
	Freight							
	Maintained Markup Projection							
	GMROI $							

		Season/Total	FEB	MAR	APR	MAY	JUN	JUL
Retail Values	Sales $							
	Sales %							
	BOM $							
	Stock/Sales Ratio #							
	EOM $							
	Markdown $							
	Markdown % of Sales							
	Markdown Distribution %							
	Sales Discounts $							
	Discount % of Sales							
	Discount Distribution %							
	Shrinkage $							
	Shrinkage % of Sales							
	Shrinkage Distribution %							
	Purchase@ Retail $							
	Cumulative Markup %							
	Average Inventory $							
	Stock Turnover #							
	Total Goods Handled @ Retail $							
	Gross Margin $							
	Gross Margin %							

		Season/Total	FEB	MAR	APR	MAY	JUN	JUL
Cost Values	Purchase@ Cost $							
	Freight Cost $							
	BOM Cost $							
	EOM Cost $							
	Total Goods Handled @ Cost $							
	Cost of Goods Sold $							

Sheet Name
File Name

Figure 1.9 Example of printed worksheet

3. Save your file as you finish *each* setup selection.

4. When you finish with the print setup, click **Save** on the Quick Access Toolbar to save your worksheet with the page setup options you applied.

5. From the Office Button menu, select **Print**. When the print window opens, check **All** as the print range, then **Active Sheet** and **OK** to start printing.

6. Your printout should look the same as that in Figure 1.9. If it does not, go back and check the print setup specifications.

2 *Excel Formulas*

Chapter Objectives

After reading this chapter, you should be able to:

▶ Use AutoSum to total values in a range.

▶ Use Excel functions to develop simple formulas.

▶ Explain the difference between relative and absolute reference.

▶ Develop a simple formula.

▶ Develop a complex formula.

▶ Explain the purpose of absolute reference.

▶ Explain the order of operations.

▶ Use selections from the formula tab to trace cell precedents and dependents.

▶ Develop a formula using an absolute reference.

▶ Use selections from the formula tab to display formula content.

▶ Set up a print view of formulas.

KEY TERMS

Absolute references are cell addresses that do not change when a formula is copied to another location.

Arguments are data used in functions. Because data are in cells, arguments are often represented by the cell reference containing data. Function arguments are displayed in parentheses, and each must be separated by a comma. A function accommodates a maximum of 30 arguments.

AutoSum is an Excel function included on the home tab that quickly sums values in a cell range. When a range is selected for AutoSum, the sum of the cells is displayed to the left, right, or below the range.

Cell ranges are groups of cells that can be adjacent or nonadjacent. Ranges are identified by the cell references.

Cell references are the unique addresses defined by the intersection of a column and a row. Cell references are used in formulas. Formulas that contain cell references automatically recalculate when cell values are changed.

Complex formulas are formulas that contains more than one operator.

Formulas are mathematical equations that are developed by users to perform mathematical operations.

Functions are Excel predefined equations for common calculations. Functions are categorized in a function library on the formula tab.

Operations are mathematical calculations such as addition, subtraction, multiplication, and division.

Operators are symbols or signs that represent a mathematical calculation. Common operators include plus (+, *add*), minus (-, *subtract*), asterisk (*, *multiply*), and forward slash (/, *divide*).

Order of operations is the sequence in which calculations are performed in a formula. The way a formula is written defines the order.

PEDMAS is an acronym for the order of operations. Operations enclosed in parentheses are performed first followed by exponents, division, multiplication, addition, and subtraction.

Relative cell references are cell addresses that change when a formula is copied to another location. When copied, a cell address in a formula automatically changes to reflect a reference relative to the address in the copied formula. *Relative* is the default reference in Excel.

Simple formulas are formulas containing one operator.

Assignments and other exercises require using Excel functions to structure formulas on worksheets to develop a dollar merchandise budget. A Formula tab is on the ribbon (see Chapter One); however, because the primary focus of this text is on retail math, this section covers Excel formulas in greater detail. The key terms listed above are related to retail math formulas that you will develop to complete assignments in this workbook.

EXCEL FORMULAS

An Excel **formula** is a mathematical equation. Formulas range from simple addition to complex formulas for statistical analyses and engineering. The advantages of using an Excel spreadsheet include the ability to:

► Use formulas to perform mathematical calculations on values in cells.

► Recalculate automatically when cell values are changed.

Advantages of using Excel spreadsheets include the ability to use functions to perform mathematical calculations and to create formulas that are dynamic. **Functions** are built-in equations that make formula writing easier. When selected, the function feature gives explanations of functions, provides parentheses to enclose the required values and syntax, and completes the formula by closing the parentheses when the argument is complete. **Arguments** are the required values for functions. When cell references instead of actual values are used as arguments, dynamic or interactive formulas are created and result in the automatic recalculation of formulas when cell values are updated with new values.

A formula tab is located on the ribbon (Figure 2.1). In addition to a function library, this tab has tools for developing formulas that range from

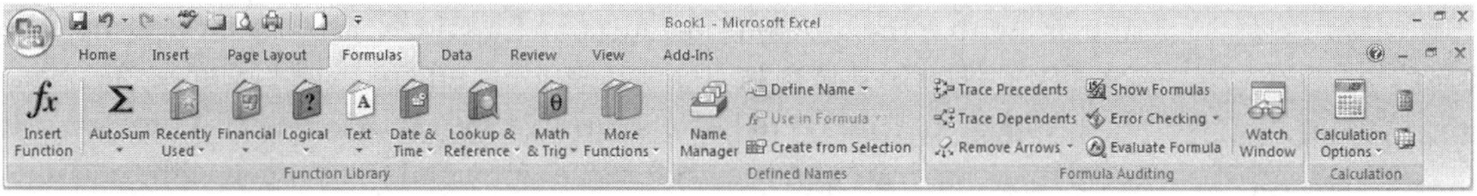

Figure 2.1 Formula tab

very simple math, such as counting, to very complex, including formulas for statistical analyses and engineering. Other formula features on the ribbon include tools for formula auditing and calculation options.

Writing a Formula

Before a formula is developed, it is important that values used in formulas and the cells where formulas will be entered are formatted correctly. Results of calculations will differ depending on how values and cells are formatted. Figure 2.2 illustrates two examples of how cell format will affect formula results. Values in cells A2 and A3 and are formatted as *general*, with no specific format.

Prior to entering a formula to sum the general values, cell A4 was formatted as *percent*. When the formula is entered, the result is displayed as a percent. In the second example, cells C2, C3, and C4 were formatted as *currency*. When the formula is entered in C4, the result is displayed as a currency. Although cells A2, A3, and A4 can be reformatted after the calculation, to guard against errors in interpreting results of calculations, cells that will contain values and formulas should be formatted *prior* to entering cells' contents.

	A	B	C
1			
2	3		$3.0
3	3		$3.0
4	600%		$6.0

Figure 2.2 Examples of how cell format affects formula results

The most commonly performed calculation is addition and Excel's **AutoSum** function eliminates manually writing this formula. The AutoSum button is located on both the home tab and formula tab (see Figure 2.1). When a range of cells is selected for AutoSum, the cells are quickly totaled and the results are displayed to the left, right, or below the range, as in Figure 2.3.

Formulas may be written to calculate cell values or Excel's built-in function feature can be used to eliminate errors associated with writing formulas. With either written formulas or functions, two basic rules must be observed. The first is to begin writing a formula in the cell where the result is to appear and always to begin a formula with an *equal* sign. A formula will contain an **operator** and cell reference. A formula developed with functions will include the function name and required arguments. The function name indicates the calculation that will be performed on the values. Depending

Figure 2.3 AutoSum totaled values included in selected range.

	A	B	C	D	E
1		FEB	MAR	APR	**Total**
2	Skirts	$2,000	$3,000	$4,000	$9,000
3	Jackets	$2,000	$3,000	$4,000	$9,000
4	Blouses	$2,000	$3,000	$4,000	$9,000
5	**Total**	$6,000	$9,000	$12,000	$27,000

on the number of operators and arguments, formulas are classified as either simple or complex.

Cell Reference

Whenever possible, formulas should be written with cell references. A **cell reference** is the address of the cell containing a value. If values in worksheets are changed, formulas containing cell references will update calculations and eliminate the need to rewrite formulas. Formulas can contain single cells or cell ranges as references. Notation of a **cell range** is two cell references, which specify the first and last cells in the range, separated by a colon. When multiple cell ranges and cell references are used in formulas, each must be separated by a comma (Figure 2.4).

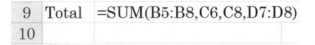

9	Total	=SUM(B5:B8,C6,C8,D7:D8)
10		

Figure 2.4 Formula containing cell ranges and single cell references

Relative Cell Reference

In formulas cells can be referenced as *relative* or *absolute*. A **relative cell reference** is a cell address that changes when a formula is copied to other locations on a worksheet. When a formula is copied, cell addresses in the formula automatically change to reflect references relative to the addresses in the copied formula. *Relative* is the default reference for Excel formulas. In Figure 2.5, the formula in cell row 9 contains all relative refer-

9	Total	=SUM(B5:B8,C6,C8,D7:D8)
10		=SUM(B6:B9,C7,C9,D8:D9)

Figure 2.5 Copied formula with relative references

ences. When the formula is copied from row 9 to row 10, the cell references change to reflect the new location.

Absolute Cell Reference

When a formula requires the same value to be used in multiple formulas, the cell reference can be written as an absolute reference. An **absolute reference** is a cell address that does not change when a formula is copied to other locations. The *F4* function key is used to make a cell reference absolute by inserting a $ in front of either or both the column and the row. In Figure 2.6, a formula in cell G5 contains an absolute reference for cell G3, which calculates a 20 percent increase of the total. When this formula is copied to cell G6, the new formula retains cell G3 as part of the formula while the relative cell references change.

Simple Formulas

A **simple formula** only has one mathematical symbol or operator. An **operation** is a mathematical calculation, such as addition, subtraction, multiplication, or division, that is performed on values. If a formula is developed without using a function feature, an operator must be used to specify the required calculation. In Figure 2.7, the simple operation of addition is performed and the plus sign is used in the formula to define *addition* as the

	F	G
1		
2		Increase
3		20.00%
4	Total	
5	$239,442	=F5+(F5*$G$3)
6	$163,253	=F6+(F6*$G$3)
7	$172,916	
8	$177,549	
9	$133,510	
10	$95,350	

Figure 2.6 Copied formula with absolute cell reference

	A	B
1		FEB
2	Skirts	$53,674
3	Jackets	$35,110
4	Blouses	$42,488
5	Pants	$40,321
6	Total	=B2+B3+B4+B5

Figure 2.7 Formula with operator and cell reference

	A	B
1		FEB
2	Skirts	$53,674
3	Jackets	$35,110
4	Blouses	$42,488
5	Pants	$40,321
6	**Total**	=SUM(B2:B5)

Figure 2.8 Excel sum function with required arguments in a cell range

	A	B	C
1			Percent Increase
2			30.0%
3		FEB	
4	Skirts	$53,674	
5	Jackets	$35,110	
6	Blouses	$42,488	
7	Pants	$40,321	
8	**Total**	$171,593	=B8+(B8*C2)

Figure 2.9 Complex formula with two operations

calculation for cells B2, B3, B4, and B5. Figure 2.8 shows an example of a formula developed with a function. Once the equal sign is entered, the **SUM** function is selected from a list and is displayed along with the required arguments for the calculation. The argument for the formula is a cell range, as shown in Figure 2.8.

Complex Formulas and the Order of Operations

A formula is complex if it contains two or more *different* operations (Figure 2.9). Excel uses a specific order for performing calculations in complex formulas. An acronym for the **order of operations** is **PEDMAS**, which means operations enclosed in parentheses are performed first, followed by exponents, division, multiplication, addition, and subtraction. However, the order of operations can be specified by using parentheses in formulas to attain desired results.

As shown in Figure 2.10, calculations following the normal order of operations produce a value of $46. However, identical cell values produce a

Figure 2.10 The order of operations changes when parentheses are used in a formula.

	A	B	C	D	E	F
1						
2	$12	$10	$4	$6	$46	=A2+B2*C2-D2
3						
4	$12	$10	$4	$6	$82	=(A4+B4)*C4-D4

value of $82 when the order of operations is changed by including cells A4 and B4 in parentheses to specify that addition be performed before multiplication and subtraction.

Formula Auditing

Once formulas are developed, Excel offers tools for checking for errors. The formula tab contains a **Formula Auditing** group with an **Error Checking** button. Two features of error checking will check formulas for common errors on a spreadsheet and will **Trace Error** sources in formulas. When errors are found, the type of error is identified and options are provided for getting help to correct the problem. When values are calculated in a cell, two additional auditing tools can be used to provide information about the formula. The **Trace Precedents** button displays arrows on the spreadsheet to show which cell or cells affect the value created by the formula. The **Trace Dependents** feature displays arrows to show which cells are affected by the cell containing the formula. When required, all formulas on a spreadsheet can be shown by using the **Show Formula** button.

Application Exercise 2.1 **Use Formulas and Functions for Calculations on a Worksheet**

In this application exercise you will use tools on the Formula tab to understand how to create formulas and use functions to perform calculations on a worksheet. Afterwards, you will use the formula auditing tools to display and evaluate your formulas.

1. Start your Excel application by selecting **Start** on your desktop to display the start menu. Then select: **Programs>Microsoft Office>Microsoft Office Excel 2007**.

2. When **Book 1** opens, immediately save it as an Excel file by selecting from the Office button menu: **Save As>Excel Workbook**. Save the file to your USB drive or desktop. Name this file *Application Exercises*. All application exercises in this workbook will be saved in this file.

3. Rename **Sheet 1** "Formulas."

4. Type and format the labels and values in the rows and columns shown in Figure 2.11.

5. Select cell range **B4:F14** and format as **currency**, **decimal place**, **0** with the **dollar sign**. Center values in cells.

Figure 2.11
Spreadsheet for
formulas and
functions to
calculate values

	A	B	C	D	E	F
1	Junior Sportswear Sales Plan by Quarter, FY 20__					
2						*What if Increase*
3		FEB	MAR	APR	**Total**	0.20
4	Skirts	531	527	518		
5	Jackets	351	393	433		
6	Blouses	180	165	324		
7	Pants	213	324	232		
8	Active Wear	213	324	234		
9	Accessories	241	325	242		
10	**Total**					
11						
12	Average					
13	Maximum					
14	Minimum					

6. Select cell **F3** and format as **percent, decimal place 1**. Center the value in the cell.

7. Select cell range **B4:E10** and click **AutoSum** on the **Formula Bar** to compute totals for the range.

8. Use the average function to calculate the average sales for FEB. Begin the formula by typing an equal sign in cell **B12**. Click the **Auto-Sum** drop down menu and select **Average**. Select the argument for the function by highlighting the cell range **B4:B9**. Enter the formula.

9. Copy the formula in cell **B12** to cells **C12:E12**.

10. Use the maximum function to calculate the maximum sales for FEB. Begin the formula by typing an equal sign in cell **B13**. Click the **Auto-Sum** drop-down menu and select **MAX**. Select the argument for the function by highlighting the cell range **B4:B9**. Enter the formula.

11. Copy the formula in Cell **B13** to Cells **C13:E13**.

12. Use the minimum function to calculate the minimum sales for FEB. Begin the formula by typing an equal sign in cell **B13**. Click the **Auto-Sum** drop-down menu and select **MIN**. Select the argument for the function by highlighting the range **B4:B9**. Enter the formula.

13. Copy the formula in cell **B14** to cells **C14:E14**.

14. Use a complex formula to calculate a 20-percent increase in the total skirts sales. In cell **F4** type the following formula:

$$= (F3 * E4) + E4$$

Enter the formula.

15. Edit the formula in cell **F4** to include an absolute reference. Double-click on cell **F4**. When the formula is displayed, place the cursor *behind* the **F3** reference and press the **F4** key on the keyboard to make the reference absolute. Enter the edited formula.

16. Copy the formula in cell **F4** to cells **F5:F9** to calculate 20-percent increases for the other items.

17. Select **Error Checking** from the formula auditing group to check formulas for errors.

18. Select cell **B12** and select **Trace Precedents** in the formula auditing group to see the cells that affect the value in cell **B12**.

19. Select cell **F3** and select **Trace Dependents** in the formula auditing group to see the cells that are affected by the value in cell **F3**.

20. Select **Remove Arrows** from the formula auditing group to remove arrows from your sheet.

21. Delete column **D**. Right-click the heading for column **D** and select **delete.**

    Note that the totals and increases in columns D and E are automatically recalculated.

22. Click the *undo* button in the quick access bar to reverse the deletion.

23. Save the file.

24. Change the percent in cell **F3** to 30 percent. *Note* that all of the values in the column are recalculated.

25. Select **Show Formulas** from the formula auditing group to display formulas in the worksheet.

26. Print the formula view of this worksheet. *Note:* If you want all your formulas to print on a single page, you should adjust the width of your columns and use *landscape* orientation.

27. When you finish printing, exit the file without saving the formula view.

3 *Planning*

Chapter Objectives

After reading this chapter you should be able to:

▶ Explain the purpose of planning.

▶ Describe planning levels in a retail organizational structure.

▶ Explain the differences in plans developed on different managerial levels.

▶ Explain the differences between an assortment plan, a promotion plan, and a sales-and-inventory plan.

▶ Explain the purpose of a profit-and-loss statement.

▶ List the basic elements of a profit-and-loss statement.

▶ Identify factors that increase and decrease the cost of sales.

▶ Explain how profit is determined.

▶ Provide a basic formula for gross margin.

▶ Explain the difference between gross margin and operating profit.

▶ List the basic steps involved in developing a merchandise budget.

KEY TERMS

Allocators are members of the merchandise division responsible for planning the distribution of inventory to individual stores to ensure the right amount, at the right location, at the right time.

Alteration/workroom expenses are costs incurred by the retailer in preparing merchandise for sale.

Assortment plans are plans for the variety, depth, and breadth of inventory to sell.

Buyers are members of the merchandise division responsible for functional planning related to inventory purchase decisions, which includes identifying resources, market visits, acquisition, pricing, and assortment planning. A buyer's role may include product development in some organizations.

The **cost of goods sold** is the cost of inventory including billed costs and transportation costs.

Department managers are members of the merchandise division responsible for planning and managing store-level activities related to selling.

Direct expenses are operating expenses that are attributable to a department in which sales occur.

Division merchandise managers (DMM) are members of the merchandise division responsible for managing and coordinating the functional planning for the buying activities of several departments in a division.

Earned cash discounts are reductions in the cost of inventory given by the vendor to the retailer for meeting specific conditions of purchase. The discount is expressed as a percent of the billed cost.

General merchandise managers (GMM) head the merchandise division and are responsible for developing corporate-level strategic plans for buying and selling.

Gross margin is the difference between sales and the *total* cost of sales. Gross margin reflects the impact of alterations and cash discounts on the inventory cost.

Gross sales are the total income received from cash and credit sales of inventory and services.

Income statements are financial reports that provide the operating results for a period in terms of profit or loss from sales, cost of goods, gross margin, and operating expenses.

Indirect expenses are general operating expenses required to support a retail organization. Indirect expenses will remain even if a sales department is eliminated.

Merchandise budgets are seasonal dollar plans, organized by months used to monitor aspects of expenditures associated with sales and inventory.

Merchandise managers are members of the merchandise division responsible for planning and coordinating store-level activities related to selling in departments.

Merchandise planning is a short-range course of action for the acquisition and sale of inventory.

Net profit is the total amount of money earned. It is calculated as operating profit plus additional income minus taxes.

Net sales are income received from the sale of inventory and services minus customer returns, discounts, and allowances. Net sales are the basis for expressing ratios on income statements.

Operating expenses are costs associated with doing business excluding those related to the acquisition of inventory.

Operating profit is the proceeds from the sale of inventory after all operating expenses are deducted.

Other expense is money deducted from the operating profit, and include things such as payment of short-term loans, dividends and interest on bonds, depreciation, and insurance.

Other income is money added to the operating profit. Other income is not generated from inventory sales, but is received in the form of interest payments from credit cards and investments and from rental income.

Planners are members of the merchandise division responsible for analyzing historical and current data to develop financial plans for sales and inventory in order to achieve financial objectives.

Planning is a process to define a course of action to accomplish specific retailing objectives.

Product developers are members of the merchandise division responsible for planning all aspects of a retailer's private-label program, including product design, specifications, sourcing, and production.

Sales are the cash or credit receipts received from the exchange of inventory or service for money.

Retail companies that sell products or services must have some type of plan in order to achieve desired objectives. An organizational structure that supports planning activities is required to achieve objectives. In approaching the topic of merchandise planning, it is important to understand how merchandise planning fits into a retail structural environment and what its role is in contributing to organizational goals.

Merchandise planning is a process related to the selection, management, and sales of inventory. Its purpose is to ensure that customers are provided with the right products, at the right place, time, and price, and in quantities that meet their needs. This implies that before merchandise plans can be developed, all aspects of their purpose—including customers, product, place, time, quantity, and price—must be defined through planning processes to ensure the intended benefits.

RETAIL ORGANIZATIONAL STRUCTURE

The discussion of planning will be approached from the standpoint of the formal organizational structure that characterizes large department stores. Retail companies assume various organizational formats depending on factors related to size, type and variety of products sold, number of locations, and number of employees. The Mazur plan, a model organizational format developed in 1927, remains the basis for department-store organization in the United States. The hierarchical structure is organized by tasks and grouped into four divisions: merchandise, publicity, store management, and control. The hierarchy reflects the reporting structures, lines of authority, communication flow, and responsibility within the retail organization (Figure 3.1).

Over time, the Mazur hierarchy gradually grew wider and steeper to include other divisions, such as human resources, marketing, catalog sales, e-commerce, and information systems, as a reflection of more contemporary approaches to retailing. Expansion of retail operations by means of branch, regional, or national multi-units required adaptations of the Mazur format based on geographic areas. These units are incorporated into organizational structures either as separate independent operations, as units of

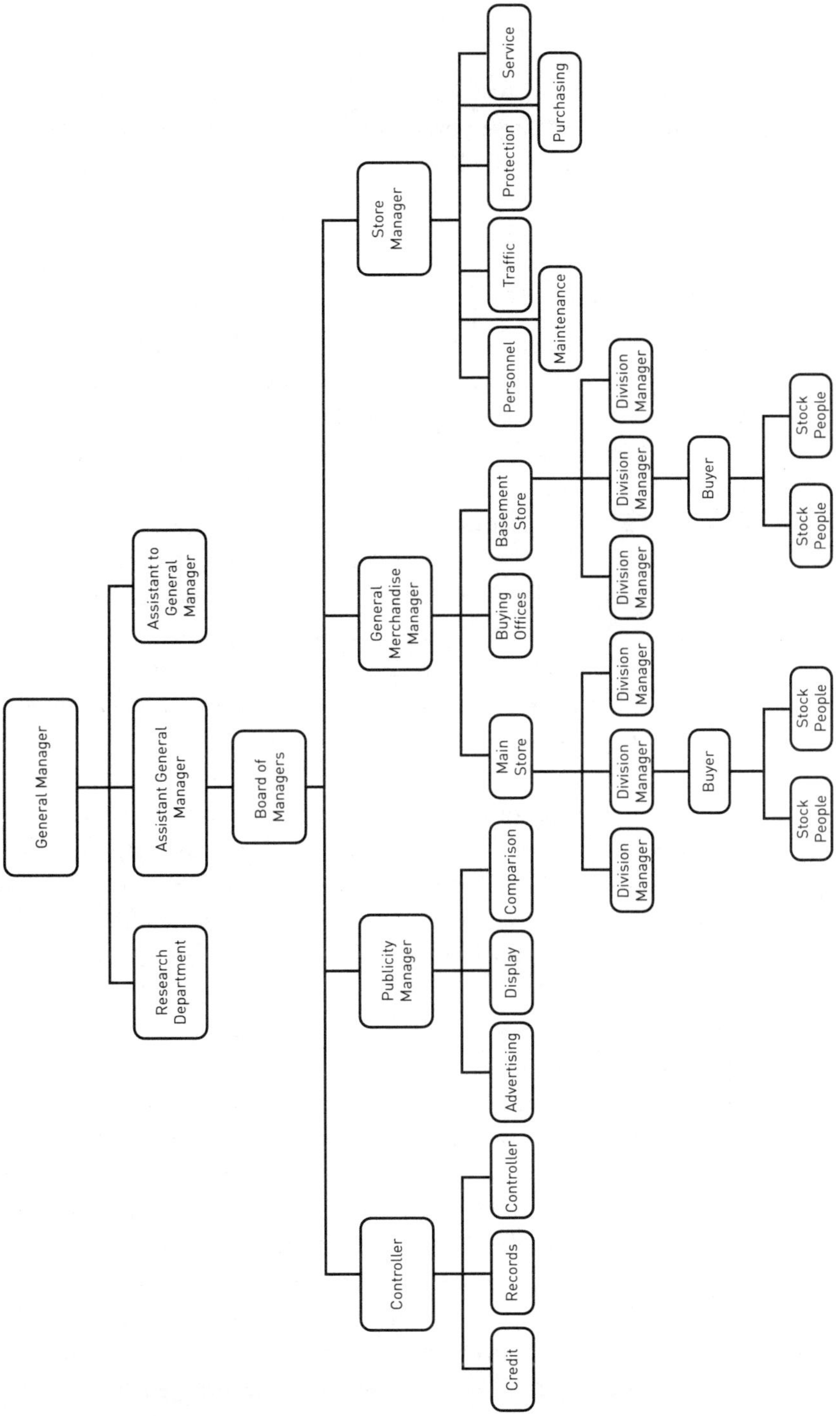

Figure 3.1 Mazur plan for retail organization

Source: Mazur, Paul (1927). *Principles of Organization Applied to Modern Retailing.* New York: Harper & Brothers.

the main store, or as equal stores. Since 1927, the structure of the merchandise division has evolved around consumer products to include divisions and departments such as *men*, *women*, and *children*, or even more concentrated departments based on product lines and price points. These changes resulted in specialized tasks related to buying and fostered the need for multilevel planning structures.

PLANNING LEVELS

In large retail firms, plans are developed at different organizational levels, including corporate, divisions, functional units, and departments. Managers at each level are responsible for developing and executing specific types of plans, all directed towards accomplishing the same mission.

Corporate-Level Plans

The chief executive officer (CEO) and other top-ranking executives at the highest corporate level plan strategically. Corporate executives assess the position of their retail organization and develop long-term goals and strategies. Strategic planning involves a process that begins with a description of the type of business and mission, which includes market segments served; its image; and statements of commitment to excellence in areas of customer relations, merchandising, marketing, and service. The mission serves as the foundation for all planning in the organization. Strategic planning requires an assessment of the economic environment and an analysis of the retailer's strengths, weaknesses, opportunities, and threats (SWOT). From this analysis, strategic plans related to marketing and financial objectives are formulated around profit, position, products, brands, size, stores, and customer base.

Division-Level Plans

In retail environments, divisions are composed of different functional units separate from each other. At this level, planning is required to integrate, coordinate, and align the functional groups' diverse activities with the corporate mission. Depending on the size of the company, individuals at this level may have different titles, including *vice president* or *general manager*. They are responsible for formulating both long-term strategic plans *and* short-term operational plans related to functional units in their divisions. Divisional plans include tactics directed towards defining, in concrete terms, how the functional operating units will accomplish corporate goals.

Functional-Unit Plans

Managers in functional units develop short-range operating plans that outline what is required to achieve long-range objectives. Each functional unit develops its own subset of specific strategies and plans consistent with the overall mission. At this level the emphasis is on planning for relatively short periods of time, ranging from six months to a year. Functional plans are related to specific product categories or classifications and are quantifiable, enabling planning results to be controlled and measured.

Department Plans

Department plans deal with specific details required to support functional-unit plans. Tactical efforts at this level must be coordinated with other departments within the organization. Typically, planning at this level involves supervision, service, and motivation of the sales force.

MERCHANDISE PLANNING

Merchandising is defined as the planning, development, and presentation of products to a target group. Inherent in this definition are specific functions associated with budgeting, inventory, assortment, sales, product development, sourcing, presentation, and promotion—all of which involve coordinated planning. A merchandise division is organized in a hierarchical structure with managerial support to direct planning for these functions.

At the top level of the merchandise division is a **general merchandise manager** (GMM) who is responsible for supervising *all* activity related to buying and selling merchandise. The second level is composed of **division merchandise managers** (DMMs) who report to the general merchandise manager. Divisional managers are responsible for monitoring sales and inventories of functional departments identified by product lines.

Other members of the merchandise division include **buyers, planners, allocators, product developers, merchandise managers**, and **department managers**. The functional tasks associated with these members are organized differently among retailers. The one common feature is that the buying and selling tasks are separate relative to where they are performed. Even though *plans* for both buying and selling are developed at the corporate level, the selling activity, as a store-level function, is supervised on-site by store managers and merchandise managers. The buying function is performed at the corporate level and managed by general and divisional managers. There are variations in how the four major activities of planning, buying, product

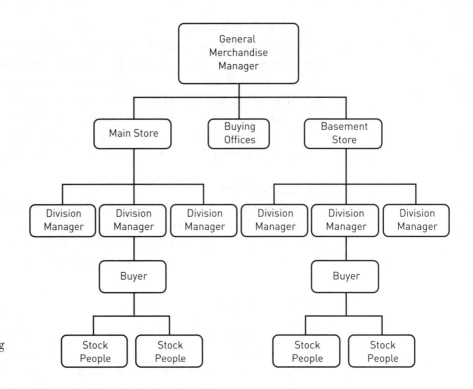

Figure 3.2a

Merchandising activities organized by stores and buying unit

development, and allocation are structured. For example, buying and planning may or may not be treated as two distinct activities. In other structural formats, planning and allocation are grouped together. Retailers with large private-label programs may organize product development as an independent unit linked with sourcing, while for less-developed programs, product development will be part of the buying function (Figure 3.2a, b, c).

Regardless of how merchandising activities are organized, coordinated planning is required to increase the probability of realizing profit. Functional planning is an ongoing activity in the merchandise division because plans must be constantly monitored, and revised sales and buying results continually evaluated.

Merchandise Plans

Three different but interrelated plans are critical for effective short-term merchandise planning. They include a sales and inventory plan, an assortment plan, and a promotion plan (Figure 3.3).

Sales results are the basis of measuring the success of merchandising activities. In order to achieve sales goals, inventory volume in units and

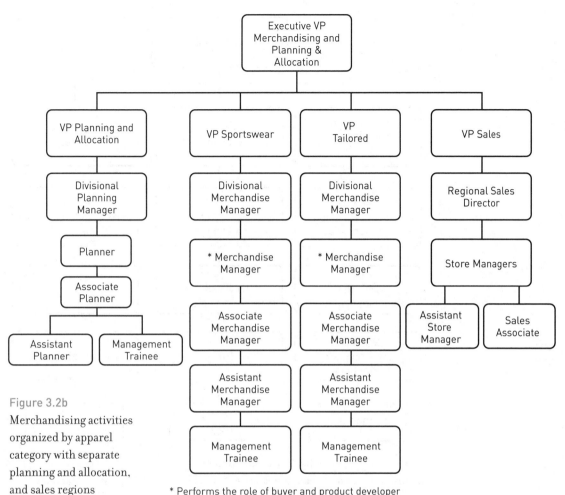

Figure 3.2b
Merchandising activities organized by apparel category with separate planning and allocation, and sales regions

* Performs the role of buyer and product developer

dollars must be available. A sales and inventory plan is designed to reconcile sales objectives with inventory requirements. Sales unit plans identify the items required to achieve sales, and inventory plans formulate budgets and purchasing plans. Through this type of plan, long-range strategic profit objectives are incorporated into a short-term budget.

Detailed assortment plans are required to select specific items to sell. An **assortment plan** focuses on the depth, variety, and breadth of an inventory, and the mix between basic and fashion items required to maximize expected profits. Short-term merchandise promotion plans in the form of advertising, in-store promotions, and displays are designed to convey the

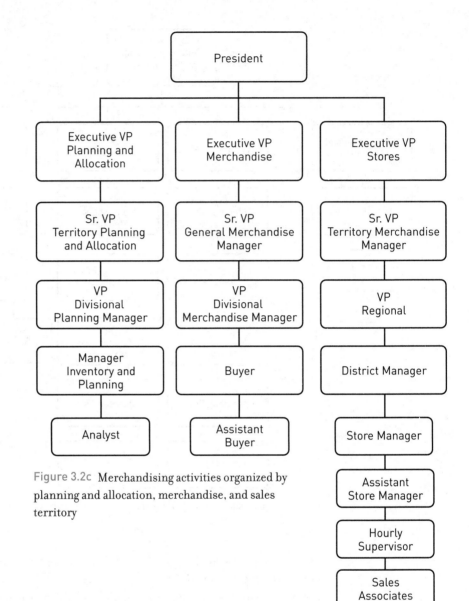

Figure 3.2c Merchandising activities organized by planning and allocation, merchandise, and sales territory

assortments offered for sale. These plans serve to maximize sales by promoting product awareness and attracting customers. Promotion planning is carried out in the division of advertising and promotion in the corporate office because detailed coordination is required with the merchandise division and other divisions.

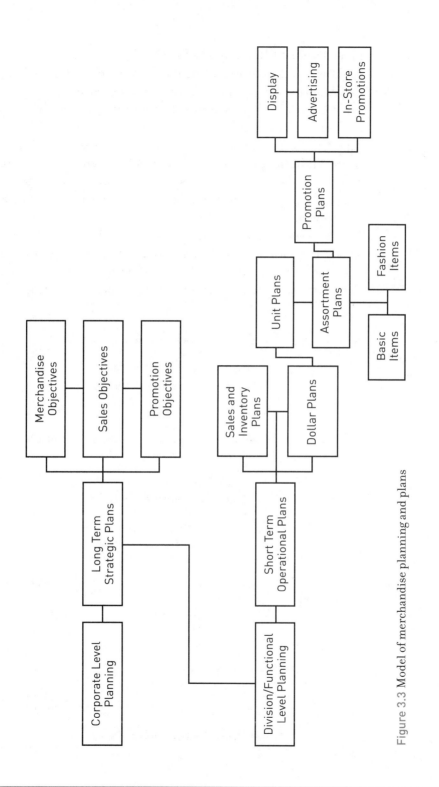

Figure 3.3 Model of merchandise planning and plans

Merchandise Planning and Profit

Profit is important in reaching the financial objectives and targets established during the planning process. Several factors determine whether a profit is realized. **Gross sales** are the dollar revenue generated from the sales of inventory before customer returns and allowances are deducted (Figure 3.4). A net sales plan is the starting point in a merchandise dollar plan and in accounting for profit or loss. **Net sales** represent the income received and serve as the basis for the expression of all profit ratios on the income statement. Net sales are important because they must support all aspects of a retail operation.

The **cost of goods sold**, which covers all costs and expenses associated with the acquisition of inventory, is an important determinant of profit. Inventory costs include the billed cost of inventory and transportation costs. The additional factors of earned cash discounts and alteration or workroom

Figure 3.4
Components of an
income statement

Components of an Income Statement

Gross Sales	
Customer Returns/Allowances	
Net Sales	**100.0%**
Cost of Goods Sold	**-50.0%**
Beginning Inventory	
Additional Inventory Purchases	
Transportation/Freight	
Total Merchandise Handled	
Ending Inventory Cost	
Cost of Goods	
Earned Cash Discounts	
Alteration/Workroom Expenses	
Gross Margin	**50.0%**
Operating Expenses	**-45.0%**
Direct Expenses	
Indirect Expenses	
Operating Profit	**5.0%**
Other Income	1.0%
Other Expenses	-2.0%
Net Profit Before Taxes	**4.0%**

expenses determine the total cost of goods sold. An **earned cash discount** is a percentage reduction in inventory cost given by the vendor for payment of the invoice within a specified time period. Cash discounts are deducted from the billed cost of the inventory to reduce the cost of sales. Discounts are important because of their potential for increasing profit. **Alteration** or **workroom expenses** represent costs related to inventory that retailers incur before and after it is sold. Examples are materials, supplies, and services related to assembling, altering, repairing, and storing merchandise purchased by customers. Retailers often pass alteration expenses on to customers. These expenses affect profits because if the entire cost is not covered by customers, alteration expenses will increase the cost of sales

As Figure 3.4 shows, gross margin is a determinant of operating profit. **Gross margin** is the difference between the total cost of goods sold and net sales. Gross margin is a first measurement of profitability because if an operating profit is to be realized, gross margin must be large enough to cover operating expenses. Because gross margin reflects profit directly attributable to the buying and selling of inventory, members of merchandising divisions are evaluated on their success in meeting their gross margin goals.

At the end of an accounting period, an **income statement** summarizes merchandising activity and provides numerical indicators that reflect whether a retailer has made a profit or sustained a loss. As shown in Figure 3.4, the income statement consists of six major components organized in sections. Sections of the income statement include subsections of monetary transactions used in calculating profit components.

Costs are categorized into two basic types, those associated with the *acquisition of inventory*, as previously discussed, and all other costs associated with running a retail business, which are **operating expenses**. Operating expenses are divided into categories of direct and indirect expenses. **Direct expenses** include expenses attributable only to the department or unit in which an inventory is sold. Direct expenses are driven by activities associated with the *sale* of inventory. If a department is eliminated, expenses associated with that department would also be eliminated. Sales associate salaries; product advertising; and administrative supplies such as postage, shipping, and delivery services are examples of direct expenses. **Indirect expenses** are not identified with a specific department but are general business expenses associated with operating a retail business. Indirect expenses will continue if a specific department is eliminated. Building leases, security, property management, utilities, maintenance, legal services, and salaries of upper management are example of indirect expenses. Both direct and indirect expenses must be controlled because profit is determined, in part, by the amount of operating expenses.

Operating profit, which is the difference between gross margin and operating expenses, is the first indicator of profitability. Operating profit reflects success in managing inventory and labor investments in retail organizations. Up to this point, all expenses are under management's control, and in instances where bonuses are paid, they are based on operating profit, which is a reflection of management's skill and ability in controlling expenses.

Net profit is the difference between operating profit, other expenses, and other income, the latter two of which are unrelated to normal selling activities. **Other expenses** include things such as payment of short-term loans, dividends and interest on bonds, depreciation, and insurance. **Other income** is money retailers receive in the form of interest from credit cards, investments, and rentals. Net profit is the income on which retailers pay income tax and is included on the income statement as net profit before taxes and net profit after taxes.

The emphasis in this workbook is on gross margin and other components previously discussed that result in operating profit or loss. Calculation of gross margin will be covered in detail in Chapter Ten. The following application exercise provides a basic formula to calculate a gross margin that illustrates the interrelationships of components that contribute to profit or loss.

Application Exercise 3.1 Calculate a Gross Margin

Start your Excel application by selecting **Start** on your desktop to display the start menu. Then select: **Programs>Microsoft Office>Microsoft Office Excel 2007**. In this exercise you will create two copies of the gross margin formula to illustrate how sales, cost of goods sold, cash discounts, and workroom expenses impact gross margin and profit.

1. Open the *Application Exercises* file that you previously saved on your USB drive or desktop.
2. Rename *Sheet 2* "Gross Margin."
3. Type only the labels and values as shown in Figure 3.5.
4. Format Column **D**, rows **3-10** as **currency, decimal place 0**.
5. Format Column **E**, rows **3-10** as **percent, decimal place 1**.

	A	B	C	D	E
1	Gross Margin Formula				
2				$	%
3		Sales		$80,000	
4	*Minus*	Cost of goods sold		$40,000	
5	*Equals*	Maintained markup			
6	*Plus*	Earned cash discounts		$5,000	
7	*Minus*	Alteration expenses		$2,000	
8	*Equals*	**Gross Margin**			
9	*Minus*	Operating expenses		$35,000	
10	*Equals*	Operating profit			

Figure 3.5 Formula for calculating gross margin

6. Use the gross margin formula shown in Column **A** and calculate dollar values for:
   - Maintained markup
   - Gross margin
   - Operating profit

   Note that it is important that you use *cell reference* in all of the formulas.

7. After you complete the formulas, select the range **B2:E10**, and copy and paste in cell **G2**. See Figure 3.6a.

8. In cells **E3** and **J3**, enter the formula to calculate percent of sales. Use an *absolute reference* in the denominator so the formula can be copied to other cells. See Figure 3.6a.

9. Copy the formulas to calculate percents in Cells **E4:E10** and **J4:J10**. See Figure 3.6b.

10. Save your file.

Now you have two GM formulas that you can use to observe the impact of profit components on gross margin and profit. You will make changes to compare the impacts.

11. In Cell **D3**, change *only* the sales *dollars* to **$100,000**.

12. In cell **I4**, change *only* the cost-of-goods-sold *dollars* to **$50,000**.

13. See Figure 3.6b.

Observe the impact on GM and profit.

14. Click "undo" *twice* to reverse the changes.

15. In cell **D9**, change *only* the operating-expenses *dollars* to **$30,000**.

16. In cell **I9**, change *only* the operating-expenses *dollars* to **$40,000**.

Observe the impact on GM and profit.

17. Click *undo* twice to reverse the changes.

18. In cell **D7**, change *only* the alteration-expense *dollars* to $0.

19. In cell **I6**, change *only* the earned cash-discounts *dollars* to $0.

20. Click *undo* twice to reverse the changes.

Notice that manipulating any of these three profit components, while holding other components constant, will impact gross margin and influence profit.

	A	B	C	D	E	F	G	H	I	J
1	Gross Margin Formula									
2				$	%				$	%
3		Sales		$80,000	=D3/$D$3		Sales		$80,000	=I3/$I$3
4	*Minus*	Cost of goods sold		$40,000			Cost of goods sold		$40,000	
5	*Equals*	Maintained markup		$40,000			Maintained markup		$40,000	
6	*Plus*	Earned cash discounts		$5,000			Earned cash discounts		$5,000	
7	*Minus*	Alteration expenses		$2,000			Alteration expenses		$2,000	
8	*Equals*	**Gross Margin**		**$43,000**			**Gross Margin**		**$43,000**	
9	*Minus*	Operating expenses		$35,000			Operating expenses		$35,000	
10	*Equals*	Operating profit		$8,000			Operating profit		$8,000	

Figure 3.6a Compare the impact of profit components on GM and profit.

	A	B	C	D	E	F	G	H	I	J
1	Gross Margin Formula									
2				$	%				$	%
3		Sales		$100,000	100.00%		Sales		$80,000	100.00%
4	*Minus*	Cost of goods sold		$40,000	40.00%		Cost of goods sold		$50,000	62.50%
5	*Equals*	Maintained markup		$60,000	60.00%		Maintained markup		$30,000	37.50%
6	*Plus*	Earned cash discounts		$5,000	5.00%		Earned cash discounts		$5,000	6.25%
7	*Minus*	Alteration expenses		$2,000	2.00%		Alteration expenses		$2,000	2.50%
8	*Equals*	**Gross Margin**		**$63,000**	63.00%		**Gross Margin**		**$33,000**	41.25%
9	*Minus*	Operating expenses		$35,000	35.00%		Operating expenses		$35,000	43.75%
10	*Equals*	Operating profit		$28,000	28.00%		Operating profit		-$2,000	-2.50%

Figure 3.6b Compare the impact of profit components on GM and profit.

MERCHANDISE BUDGETS

A **merchandise budget** is an estimate of future sales and inventory requirements for a category of merchandise. Its purpose is to guide the purchasing or investment in inventory. Two merchandising concepts—planning and control—are reflected in a merchandise budget. The budget outlines plans for dollar investment, and a limit on investment is introduced through retail-math formulas to arrive at budgetary figures. The dollar plan monitors all aspects of expenditures and profit associated with sales and inventory and establishes quantitative benchmarks for evaluating the success of merchandising activities.

A merchandise budget is a seasonal functional plan. Traditionally, because of the amount of time required for producing and transporting inventory to the place of sale, most merchandise budgets were developed for two 6-month seasons, spring and fall, with budgetary projections by month. Some retailers develop an annual budget while others plan budgets for shorter time periods to reflect the merchandising seasons of products. Although the budgetary time frame varies, the components of a merchandise budget are the same in bringing together elements related to sales and inventory.

STEPS IN DEVELOPING A DOLLAR MERCHANDISE BUDGET

Topics and activities in this workbook relate to developing a merchandise dollar plan using retail-math formulas and principles. The merchandise budget plan will be developed in seven activities in this workbook and will include calculating a variety of evaluative measures related to sales and inventory including:

- ▶ A sales plan
- ▶ An inventory plan
- ▶ A reductions plan
- ▶ A plan for purchases retail value
- ▶ A plan of initial markup and maintained markup
- ▶ A plan for purchases' cost values
- ▶ A plan for cost of sales

Afterwards, an amplified gross margin statement will be developed to illustrate how variables in the merchandise budget are used to calculate a gross margin.

4 *Sales Planning*

Chapter Objectives

After reading this chapter you should be able to:

▶   Explain the importance of sales planning.

▶   Describe quantitative methods used to project sales.

▶   Explain the importance of using qualitative inputs to plan sales.

▶   Structure simple and complex formulas in Excel to calculate:

- percent change in sales
- percent increase in sales
- percent decrease in sales
- dollar distributions of total sales volume

▶   Develop a sales plan.

KEY TERMS

Bottom-up sales planning is a method of planning sales in which functional units and departments generate sales projections that are rolled up into a total projection for the organization.

A **fashion trend** is the direction in which fashion is moving as determined by subjective evaluations of commonalities in consumer preferences.

Last year–minus is a method of projecting sales in which a percent is subtracted from last season's sales to arrive at a sales value for the next season.

Last year–plus is a method of projecting sales in which a percent is added to last season's sales to arrive at a sales value for the next season.

Regression analysis is a statistical method of forecasting sales. Historical sales data are used to identify and weigh factors that impacted past sales, and those factors are then applied to projections of future sales.

Sales are revenue derived from the sale of inventory.

Sales plans are documents prepared prior to the beginning of a season that specify the total season's sales objectives and schedule future sales by month or weeks.

Sales trends illustrate the growth patterns of sales as determined by calculations of percent change in sales volume over time.

Time series is a method of projecting sales that uses trend data to project sales. This method assumes that what happened in past seasons is likely to occur in the future.

Top-down sales planning is a method of planning sales in which the sales projection for an entire organization is set by corporate and senior-level division managers.

Trend is a general tendency or directional movement determined by observation.

In the previous chapters you developed an understanding of how to use the latest version of Excel to structure formulas and the importance of planning in a retail organization. We will now begin the first stage of developing a six-month dollar plan using Excel and the planning form that you completed in

Chapter One. Your first assignment leading to the completion of a sales plan appears at the end of this chapter.

SALES

A **sales plan** is a forecast of revenue that will be derived from the sale of inventory. A forecast of a total season's sales volume is the first step in developing a short-term merchandise dollar plan. This initial step is the most important aspect of planning because decisions related to inventory investment and control rely on accurate sales projections.

Obtaining initial sales projections from each level of the merchandise division is a common starting point for planning sales. This approach uses **top-down** and **bottom–up sales planning** to divide sales estimates into segments. The top corporate executives forecast total–sales projections for the entire organization. Sales projections at this level are based on broad corporate objectives formulated during the strategic planning process. The corporate total is then subdivided among the divisions of the organization. The bottom-up sales planning approach requires functional units and departments in each merchandising division to generate sales projections. Forecasts at bottom levels are based on recent sales records in addition to observations and experience gained through close contact with products and customers. Projections from top-down and bottom-up segments are then combined and reconciled among divisions and departments to arrive at a total–sales projection for the entire organization.

DEVELOPING SALES PROJECTIONS

Reliable sales projection methods are required at any level of an organization to guard against the decrease in profit that will result from lost sales when inventory levels do not match demand. Sales planning is both an art and a science, requiring qualitative and quantitative input. Intuition, judgment, and experience contribute to the art, while figures and mathematical skill contribute to the science of sales planning.

Quantitative Methods for Planning Sales
Several sales planning methods used by retailers incorporate the quantitative aspects of planning. The accuracy varies depending on methods used. The most common quantitative methods are forecasting future sales based

on past sales, employing statistical methods using regression, and a combination of these two.

Last Year–Plus or Last Year–Minus

Common methods used to forecast sales are **last year–plus** or **last year–minus**. These are simple methods that use the last "like" season's sales volume to establish the next season's forecast. A percent is *added to* or *subtracted from* the last season's sales results. The planner uses qualitative input from the retail environment in determining the percent increase or decrease. Because only one season is used in the forecast, qualitative input is important to finalize the projection.

Time Series Method

Time series uses trends to project sales and requires an examination of previous seasons' sales records. The number of previous seasons to include in the forecast is determined by managerial judgment and experience. With this method, like seasons and like products must be used for accurate forecasts. This approach assumes that what happened in past seasons is likely to occur in the future. For example, holidays, weather patterns, and back-to-school shopping affect sales volume in similar ways from year to year. Using numerical data that reflect these demands, along with monthly sales variations over several seasons and calculations of variance and averages will reveal trends on which future sales are projected.

Regression Analysis

Regression analysis is a statistical sales planning method that starts with historical data from the last year and uses a number of variables statistically identified as influencing the retailer's sales. Variables include factors related to the number of selling days or holidays, demographics, advertising, population change, and disposable income. Variables are assigned weights according to their impact on sales and are introduced into a statistical model to calculate a sales estimate. The more variables used in the model, the more accurate the sales projection.

Combination of Methods

An integrated approach to forecasting sales includes using time series, last year–plus, or regression analysis, in combination with other forecasts such as marketing or financial data. Some retailers take advantage of weather forecasting technology to increase planning accuracy by integrating long-range weather forecasts into planning sales for weather-dependent merchandise.

Qualitative Input for Planning Sales

The primary limitation of quantitative forecasting methods is that they cannot stand alone as the sole determinant of sales projections. Intuition and gut-level feelings about fashion and products are as important in developing and supporting sales plans as are knowledge of consumers and the retail environment.

Fashion Trends

Fashion is defined as the accepted style or custom at a given point in time. A **trend** is a general tendency or directional movement. Trends are determined by observing what people are wearing, doing, or saying. Because trends are reflected in retail sales, they can reinforce sales projections if retailers are able to anticipate consumer interest in new products and services. Experienced retailers look to customers and to current and social events for trends. Trend resources exhibitions, reports by national and international designers, trade shows, and trend forecasting agencies provide projections for colors, fabrics, and designs with a forecast range of six months to one year.

Product Knowledge

Products have a life cycle that progresses from introduction through growth, maturity, decline, and obsolescence. To determine where current products fall in the life cycle, and when they will enter the next stage of life, requires looking forward and combining subjective judgments of current and future cycles. Products are classified as *staple*, *basic*, *fashion*, and *fad*. Projecting sales for staple and basic products may be easier because sales are less volatile and can be forecast with higher degrees of accuracy. Fashion and fad products are more difficult to plan because of their life cycle and the lack of historical records on which to base sales and inventory requirements. Planning must include an awareness of all of these product characteristics in order to be successful.

Retail Environment

While some aspects of a retail environment can be quantified, most require retailers' individual subjective assessments of the impacts that environmental changes will have on their sales. Factors related to store attributes, competition, acquisitions and mergers, online and catalog shopping, and local and global economic conditions impact how sales are forecast.

PLANNING A TOTAL SEASON'S SALES

A total-season-dollar-sales value is planned first. Next, the total is divided into parts and distributed over the number of weeks or months in the season.

Sales planning requires an examination of previous sales. A comparison of dollar values shows whether sales have increased or decreased from one period to another. Because dollar values vary, a more meaningful comparison is the percent of change from one period to another. Percent changes between previous periods can be used as a starting point for planning future sales.

Calculating a Percent Change

Percent change is an increase or decrease in value between two periods. A percent change can be calculated for any two periods. Formulas for calculating a percent change are as follows:

$$\text{Percent Change} = \frac{\text{Current Period} - \text{Prior Period}}{\text{Prior Period}}$$

Alternate Formula:

$$\text{Percent Change} = \frac{\text{Current Period}}{\text{Prior Period}} - 1$$

Both formulas yield the same result. In the first formula, the percent is based on how much the resulting difference between the two periods varies from the prior period. The alternate formula assumes the prior period as 100 percent and the percent change is based on how much the current period varies from 100.

Application Exercise 4.1 Use Formulas to Calculate a Percent Change

Figures 4.1a, 4.1b, and 4.1c illustrate use of the two complex formulas to calculate percent change. You will use these formulas to calculate the percent change in units for shirts sold in 2007 and shirts with different collar styles sold in 2008.

---

1. Open your *Application Exercises* file.

2. Insert a blank worksheet by clicking on the drop-down menu on the **Insert** button in the cells group or by holding down the Shift key and pressing *F11*.

3. Type in the values and labels shown in Figure 4.1a.

4. Format cell range **D8:E10** as **percent, decimal place 1**.

5. Enter the formula in cell **D8** to calculate the percent change between 2007 and 2008, as shown in Figure 4.1b.

   Note that in applying the formula for percent change, the *current* period is the most recent period.

6. Enter the alternate formula in cell **E8**.

   Note the order of operations in the formula structures.

7. Copy the formula to rows **9** and **10** to calculate the percent change for point- and spread-collar shirts (Figure 4.1c).

8. Rename the sheet *Percent Change*.

9. Save your file.

Figure 4.1a
Formulas for calculating percent change

	A	B	C	D	E
1	*Calculate Percent Change*				
2	*(Current Period - Prior Period) / Prior Period*				
3	*Alternate Formula*				
4	*(Current Period / Prior Period) -1*				
5					
6		**2008**	**2007**	**% Change**	**% Change**
7	**Collar Styles**	**Unit Sales**	**Unit Sales**		
8	*Button Down*	60,201	142,131	?	?
9	*Point Collar*	131,000	175,606	?	?
10	*Spread Collar*	217,907	200,000	?	?

Figure 4.1b
Formulas for calculating percent change

	A	B	C	D	E
6		**2008**	**2007**	**% Change**	**% Change**
7	**Collar Styles**	**Unit Sales**	**Unit Sales**		
8	*Button Down*	60,201	142,131	=(B8-C8)/C8	=(B8/C8)-1
9	*Point Collar*	131,000	175,606	?	?
10	*Spread Collar*	217,907	200,000	?	?

Figure 4.1c

Formulas for
calculating percent
change

	A	B	C	D	E
6		**2008**	**2007**	**% Change**	**% Change**
7	**Collar Styles**	**Unit Sales**	**Unit Sales**		
8	*Button Down*	60,201	142,131	-57.6%	-57.6%
9	*Point Collar*	131,000	175,606	-25.4%	-25.4%
10	*Spread Collar*	217,907	200,000	9.0%	9.0%

As shown in Figure 4.1c, calculations of percent change show unit sales for button-down and point-collar shirts decreased while unit sales for spread-collar shirts increased between 2007 and 2008. Figure 4.1c also shows that both formulas yield the same result.

Application Exercise 4.2 Calculate a Percent Change to Show a Sales Trend

By linking calculations of percent change together for successive periods, a sales trend can be revealed. The trend can be used as the basis for planning future sales.

You will use a complex formula to calculate percent change over multiple seasons.

1. Open your *Application Exercises* file.

2. Insert a blank worksheet by clicking on the insert sheet button or by holding down the Shift key and pressing *F11*.

3. Type and format the values and labels as shown in Figure 4.2a.

4. Format cell **D7:D12** as **percent, decimal place 1**. Format cell **B12** as **currency, decimal place 0**.

5. Enter the formula in cell **D7** to calculate the percent change between seasons.

6. Use the fill handle to copy the formula to cells **D8:D12** to calculate the percent change for the remaining seasons (Figure 4.2b).

7. Rename the sheet *Sales Trend*.

8. Save your file.

In Figure 4.2b, the percent-change formula reveals a trend of modest increases over the seasons. A value of -100 percent is calculated in cell D12 because sales for Fall 2010 have not been planned and are zero, or 100 percent less than Fall 2009 sales.

Figure 4.2a Percent
change between
seasons

	A	B	C	D
1	*Calculate Percent Change*			
2	*(Current Period - Prior Period) / Prior Period*			
3	*Alternate Formula*			
4	*(Current Period / Prior Period) -1*			
5				
6	**Seasons**	**Current**	**Previous**	**% Change**
7	Fall 2004/2005	$35,997	$35,530	=(B7-C7)/C7
8	Fall 2005/2006	$36,500	$35,997	?
9	Fall 2006/2007	$37,000	$36,500	?
10	Fall 2007/2008	$37,851	$37,000	?
11	Fall 2008/2009	$38,812	$37,851	?
12	Fall 2009/2010		$38,812	?

Figure 4.2b Percent
change between
seasons

	A	B	C	D
6	**Seasons**	**Current**	**Previous**	**% Change**
7	Fall 2004/2005	$35,997	$35,530	1.3%
8	Fall 2005/2006	$36,500	$35,997	1.4%
9	Fall 2006/2007	$37,000	$36,500	1.4%
10	Fall 2007/2008	$37,851	$37,000	2.3%
11	Fall 2008/2009	$38,812	$37,851	2.5%
12	Fall 2009/2010		$38,812	-100.0%

Application Exercise 4.3 Develop an Excel Chart to Show a Sales Trend Line

In this exercise you will create an Excel chart on the *Sales Trend* sheet to illustrate the trend line.

1. Open your *Application Exercises* file.
2. Select cells **A7:A12** and while holding the **Ctrl** key select cells **B7:B12**.
3. Click on the **Insert** tab and select **Line** from the **Charts** group.
4. Select a **3D line** chart to display the sales trend line. Delete the legend (Figure 4.3a).
5. Enlarge the chart by clicking and dragging either part of the frame.
6. Save your file.

Figure 4.3a Charts
illustrating sales
trend lines

	A	B	C	D	E
6	**Seasons**	**Current**	**Previous**	**% Change**	
7	Fall 2004/2005	$35,997	$35,530	1.3%	
8	Fall 2005/2006	$36,500	$35,997	1.4%	
9	Fall 2006/2007	$37,000	$36,500	1.4%	
10	Fall 2007/2008	$37,851	$37,000	2.3%	
11	Fall 2008/2009	$38,812	$37,851	2.5%	
12	Fall 2009/2010		$38,812	-100.0%	
13					

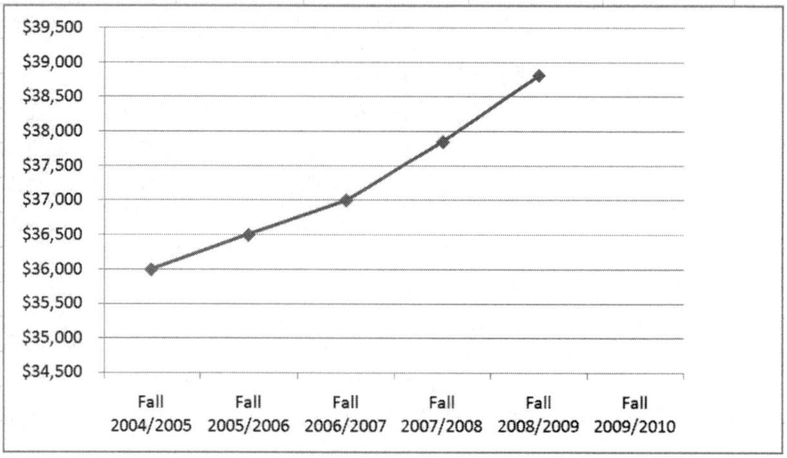

Figure 4.3b Charts
illustrating sales
trend lines

	A	B	C	D	E
6	**Seasons**	**Current**	**Previous**	**% Change**	
7	Fall 2004/2005	$35,997	$35,530	1.3%	
8	Fall 2005/2006	$36,500	$35,997	1.4%	
9	Fall 2006/2007	$37,000	$36,500	1.4%	
10	Fall 2007/2008	$37,851	$37,000	2.3%	
11	Fall 2008/2009	$38,812	$37,851	2.5%	
12	Fall 2009/2010	$37,827	$38,812	-2.5%	
13					

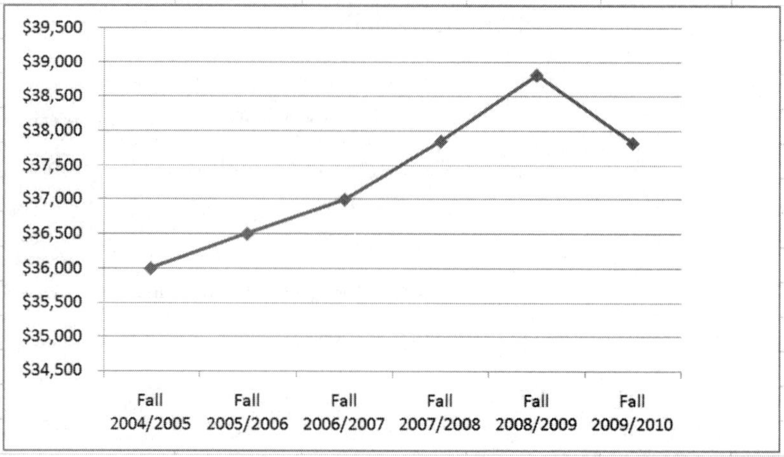

Figure 4.3c Charts illustrating sales trend lines

	Seasons	Current	Previous	% Change
6	**Seasons**	**Current**	**Previous**	**% Change**
7	Fall 2004/2005	$35,997	$35,530	1.3%
8	Fall 2005/2006	$36,500	$35,997	1.4%
9	Fall 2006/2007	$37,000	$36,500	1.4%
10	Fall 2007/2008	$37,851	$37,000	2.3%
11	Fall 2008/2009	$38,812	$37,851	2.5%
12	Fall 2009/2010	$38,812	$38,812	0.0%

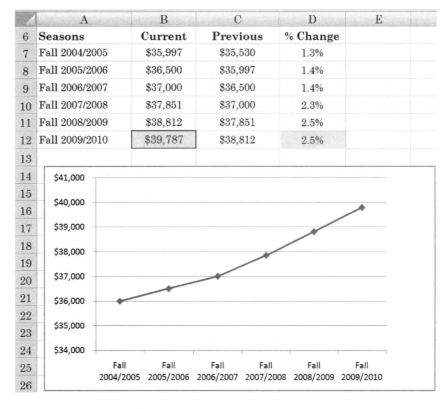

Figure 4.3d Charts illustrating sales trend lines

	Seasons	Current	Previous	% Change
6	**Seasons**	**Current**	**Previous**	**% Change**
7	Fall 2004/2005	$35,997	$35,530	1.3%
8	Fall 2005/2006	$36,500	$35,997	1.4%
9	Fall 2006/2007	$37,000	$36,500	1.4%
10	Fall 2007/2008	$37,851	$37,000	2.3%
11	Fall 2008/2009	$38,812	$37,851	2.5%
12	Fall 2009/2010	$39,787	$38,812	2.5%

Note: Because Cell B12 is included in the chart range, what is entered into cell B12 will *either* maintain the sales projection for Fall 2010, continue its upward trend, or reverse it downward.

7.   Insert **\$37,827** into cell **B12** and notice that a downward trend line for Fall 2009/2010 is reflected in the chart because fewer sales are planned for the current season than for the previous season (Figure 4.3b).

8.   Next, insert **\$38,812** into cell **B12** and notice that the trend line is maintained because sales for Fall 2010 are planned at the same level as for Fall 2009 (Figure 4.3c).

9.   Insert **\$39,787** into cell **B12** and notice that an upward trend line is continued for Fall 2009/2010 (Figure 4.3d).

10.   Save your file.

Calculating an Increase in Sales

Adding or subtracting a specific percentage from last season's sales is a common way of planning a future season's sales value. The formula for calculating a sales increase is as follows:

Sales Increase = Last Season's Sales + (Last Season's Sales * Percent Increase)

Application Exercise 4.4 Structure a Simple Formula to Calculate a Sales Increase

In Application Exercise 4.3, sales were *estimated* for Fall 2010 simply by inserting values into cell B12. This exercise demonstrates how to structure two simple formulas to *calculate* an increased sales value.

1.   Open your *Applications Exercises* file.

2.   Insert a blank worksheet by clicking on the insert sheet button or by holding down the Shift key and pressing *F11*.

3.   Type and format the values and labels as shown in Figure 4.4a.

4.   Format cells **C5** and **D5** as **currency, decimal place 0.**

5.   Type the simple formula in cell **C5** to calculate the dollar increase (Figure 4.4b).

6.   Now type another simple formula in cell **D5** to add the dollar amount of increase to Fall 2009 (last year's, or *LY*) sales (Figure 4.4c and Figure 4.4d).

7.   Rename the sheet *Calculate Sales Increase*.

8.   Save your file.

Figure 4.4a Simple
formulas for
calculating a sales
increase

	A	B	C	D
1	*Calculate Increase in Sales*			
2	*Last Season + (Last Season * Percent Increase)*			
3				
4	**Fall 2009 Sales (LY)**	**Percent of Increase**	**Dollar Amount of Increase**	**Fall 2010 Sales Plan**
5	$38,812	2.5%	?	?

Figure 4.4b Simple
formulas for
calculating a sales
increase

	A	B	C	D
4	**Fall 2009 Sales (LY)**	**Percent of Increase**	**Dollar Amount of Increase**	**Fall 2010 Sales Plan**
5	$38,812	2.5%	=A5*B5	?

Figure 4.4c Simple
formulas for
calculating a sales
increase

	A	B	C	D
1	*Calculate increase in sales*			
2	*Last season + (Last season * Percent increase)*			
3				
4	**Fall 2009 sales (LY)**	**Percent of increase**	**Dollar amount of increase**	**Fall 2010 sales plan**
5	$38,812	2.5%	$970	=C5+A5

Figure 4.4d Simple
formulas for
calculating a sales
increase

	A	B	C	D
4	**Fall 2009 Sales (LY)**	**Percent of Increase**	**Dollar Amount of Increase**	**Fall 2010 Sales Plan**
5	$38,812	2.5%	$970	$39,782

Application Exercise 4.5 Structure a Complex Formula to Calculate a Sales Increase

In this exercise you will calculate an increase in sales using one complex formula.

1. Open your *Application Exercises* file and use the *Calculate Sales Increase* sheet.

2. Copy and paste row 5 to row 7 (Figure 4.5a).

3. Delete the formulas in cells C7 and D7.

4. Enter the complex formula in cell D7 to calculate an increase in Fall 2009 sales (Figures 4.5a and 4.5b).

5. Save your file.

As shown in Figure 4.5b, total sales values planned for Fall 2010 are the same when using simple or complex formulas. However, with a complex formula,

Figure 4.5a
Complex formula for
calculating a sales
increase

	A	B	C	D
1	*Calculate Increase in Sales*			
2	*Last Season + (Last Season * Percent Increase)*			
3				
4	**Fall 2009 Sales (LY)**	**Percent of Increase**	**Dollar Amount of Increase**	**Fall 2010 Sales Plan**
5	$38,812	2.5%	**$970**	**$39,782**
6				
7	$38,812	2.5%		=A7+(A7*B7)

Figure 4.5b
Complex formula for
calculating a sales
increase

	A	B	C	D
4	**Fall 2009 Sales (LY)**	**Percent of Increase**	**Dollar Amount of Increase**	**Fall 2010 Sales Plan**
5	$38,812	2.5%	**$970**	**$39,782**
6				
7	$38,812	2.5%		$39,782

only one cell is required for the formula because the dollar increase is not shown but is calculated in parentheses before being added to Fall 2009 (LY) sales.

Calculating a Decrease in Sales

The formula for calculating a sales decrease is as follows:

Sales Decrease = Last Season's Sales – (Last Season's Sales * Percent Decrease)

Application Exercise 4.6 Structure a Simple Formula to Calculate a Sales Decrease

In this exercise you will calculate a percent decrease in sales. The calculation is structured with two simple formulas.

1. Open your *Applications Exercises* file.

2. Insert a blank worksheet by clicking on the insert sheet button or by holding down the Shift key and pressing *F11*.

3. Type and format the values and labels as shown in Figure 4.6a.

4. Format cells **C5** and **D5** as **currency**, **decimal place 0**.

5. Type the simple formula in cell **C5** to calculate the dollar decrease (Figure 4.6b).

6. Type the simple formula in cell **D5** to subtract the dollar amount of decrease from Fall 2009 sales (LY; Figures 4.6c and 4.6d).

7. Rename the sheet *Calculate Sales Decrease*.

8. Save your file.

Figure 4.6a Simple formulas for calculating a sales decrease

	A	B	C	D
1	*Calculate Decrease in Sales*			
2	*Last Season - (Last Season * Percent Decrease)*			
3				
4	**Fall 2009 Sales (LY)**	**Percent of Decrease**	**Dollar Amount of Decrease**	**Fall 2010 Sales Plan**
5	$38,812	2.5%	?	?

Figure 4.6b Simple formulas for calculating a sales decrease

	A	B	C	D
4	**Fall 2009 Sales (LY)**	**Percent of Decrease**	**Dollar Amount of Decrease**	**Fall 2010 Sales Plan**
5	$38,812	2.5%	=B5*A5	?
6				

Figure 4.6c Simple formulas for calculating a sales decrease

	A	B	C	D
4	**Fall 2009 Sales (LY)**	**Percent of Decrease**	**Dollar Amount of Decrease**	**Fall 2010 Sales Plan**
5	$38,812	2.5%	$970	=A5-C5

Figure 4.6d Simple formulas for calculating a sales decrease

	A	B	C	D
4	**Fall 2009 Sales (LY)**	**Percent of Decrease**	**Dollar Amount of Decrease**	**Fall 2010 Sales Plan**
5	$38,812	2.5%	$970	$37,842

Application Exercise 4.7 Structure a Complex Formula to Calculate a Sales Decrease

In this exercise you will calculate a decrease in sales with one complex formula.

1. Open your *Application Exercises* file and use the *Calculate Sales Decrease* sheet.

2. Copy and paste row 5 to row 7 (Figure 4.7a).

3. Delete the formulas in cells C7 and D7.

4. Enter the complex formula in cell D7 to calculate a decrease from Fall 2009 sales for Fall 2010 (Figure 4.7a).

5. Save your file.

As shown in Figure 4.7b, the values for decreased sales for Fall 2010 are the same when using simple or complex formulas.

Figure 4.7a
Complex formula for
calculating a sales
decrease

	A	B	C	D
4	**Fall 2009 Sales (LY)**	**Percent of Decrease**	**Dollar Amount of Decrease**	**Fall 2010 Sales Plan**
5	$38,812	2.5%	**$970**	**$37,842**
6				
7	$38,812	2.5%		=A7-(A7*B7)

Figure 4.7b
Complex formula for
calculating a sales
decrease

	A	B	C	D
4	**Fall 2009 Sales (LY)**	**Percent of Decrease**	**Dollar Amount of Decrease**	**Fall 2010 Sales Plan**
5	$38,812	2.5%	**$970**	**$37,842**
6				
7	$38,812	2.5%		$37,842

In structuring a complex formula for calculating a sales decrease, the order of operations is very important. Because subtraction is one of the operations, last year's sales must *precede* the part of the formula that calculates the dollar decrease (Figure 4.7a).

PLANNING DISTRIBUTIONS OF A TOTAL SEASON'S SALES

After a total-season sales estimate is determined, a plan must be developed for distributing the total sales over a product category or season. For example, a total-department sales figure must be divided into sales estimates for various products in the department. Likewise, a season's total-sales figure must be divided into separate estimates for weekly or monthly sales in the season. Sales distributions are planned as percents of the total planned sales value. Because the season's total sales represent 100 percent, the distribution percents when added, must equal 100 percent.

Calculating Percent-to-Total Sales

Planning distributions of total-season sales requires analysis of the previous season's sales distributions. Last season's distribution percents are then adjusted to reflect anticipated changes. Percent-to-total is a calculation that shows how a total-sales figure was distributed among its parts. The percents by which total sales were distributed the previous season are the starting point in planning sales distributions for a future season. The following formula is used to calculate percent-to-total.

$$\text{Percent-to-Total} = \text{Part/Total}$$

This formula can be used to calculate percent-to-total dollars or percent-to-total units. It can be used, for example, to calculate the percent of a month's sales to the sales of the total season, department sales to total store sales, category sales to total department sales, class sales to total category sales, a week's sales to the total month's sales, and a month's sales to the sales for a total year.

Application Exercise 4.8 Calculate Percent-to-Total Sales

In this exercise you will calculate the percents that four departments' sales represented to the total-store sales in a previous season. An absolute reference will be used in a simple formula.

1. Open your *Application Exercises* file.

2. Insert a blank worksheet and type and format the values and labels as shown in Figure 4.8a.

3. Format cell range **C7:C13** as **percent, decimal place 1**.

4. Enter formulas in cells **B13** and **C13** to sum values that will be calculated. Note that cells can be summed prior to entering values into the cells (Figure 4.8a).

5. Enter the formula in cell **C7** to calculate the percent-to-total sales.

    Note that the total-store sales value in cell **B13** is an absolute value (Figure 4.8b).

6. Copy the formula to cells **C8:C11** to calculate the percent of sales for the other departments.

    Note that percents for the five departments total 100 percent in cell **C13** (Figure 4.8c).

7. Rename the sheet *Percent to Total*.

8. Save your file.

Calculating Sales Distributions

Once previous sales distributions are examined and decisions are made as to how to distribute sales on a percentage basis, the dollar values that the percents represent can be calculated. The formula for calculating dollar distributions is as follows:

Dollar Distributions = Total (dollars or units) * Percent-to-Total

Figure 4.8a

Formula for
calculating percent-
to-total sales

	A	B	C
1	**Calculate Percent-to-Total Sales**		
2	*Part $ / Total*		
3			
4		Fall 2009	
5			**Percent to Total**
6		$	%
7	Department 1	$51,592	?
8	Department 2	$49,228	?
9	Department 3	$91,362	?
10	Department 4	$41,650	?
11	Department 5	$34,878	?
12			
13	**Total Store**	**=SUM(B7:B11)**	**=SUM(C7:C11)**

Figure 4.8b

Formula for
calculating percent-
to-total sales

	A	B	C
5			**Percent to Total**
6		$	%
7	Department 1	$51,592	=B7/$B$13
8	Department 2	$49,228	?
9	Department 3	$91,362	?
10	Department 4	$41,650	?
11	Department 5	$34,878	?
12			
13	**Total Store**	**$268,710**	**0.0%**

Figure 4.8c

Formula for
calculating percent-
to-total sales

	A	B	C
5			**Percent to Total**
6		$	%
7	Department 1	$51,592	**19.2%**
8	Department 2	$49,228	**18.3%**
9	Department 3	$91,362	**34.0%**
10	Department 4	$41,650	**15.5%**
11	Department 5	$34,878	**13.0%**
12			
13	**Total Store**	**$268,710**	**100.0%**

Application Exercise 4.9 Calculate the Dollar Distribution of Sales

In this exercise you will calculate the distribution of total-sales dollars using a simple formula with an absolute reference.

1.   Open your *Application Exercise* file.

2.   Insert a blank worksheet and type and format the values and labels as shown in Figure 4.9a.

3.   Format cells B7:B11 as **currency, decimal place 0.**

4.   Enter the formula in cell **C13** to sum percents.

     Note that percents will total 100 percent (Figure 4.9b).

5.   Enter the formula in cell **B7** to calculate the dollar distribution.

     Note that the total-store-sales value in cell **B13** is an absolute value (Figure 4.9b).

6.   Copy the formula to cells **B8:B11** to calculate dollar values for other departments (Figure 4.9c).

7.   Rename the sheet *Dollar Distributions*.

8.   Save your file.

Figure 4.9a

Formula for dollar distributions of total sales

	A	B	C
1	*Calculate Total Dollar Distributions*		
2	*Distribution Percent * Total Sales*		
3			
4	Fall 2010		
5			Percent of Sales
6		$	%
7	Department 1	?	18.3%
8	Department 2	?	34.6%
9	Department 3	?	18.8%
10	Department 4	?	21.3%
11	Department 5	?	7.0%
12			
13	Total Store	$322,452	?

Figure 4.9b

Formula for dollar
distributions of total
sales

	A	B	C
5			Percent of Sales
6		$	%
7	Department 1	=C7*$B$13	18.3%
8	Department 2	?	34.6%
9	Department 3	?	18.8%
10	Department 4	?	21.3%
11	Department 5	?	7.0%
12			
13	Total Store	$322,452	100.0%

Figure 4.9c

Formula for dollar
distributions of total
sales

	A	B	C
5			Percent of Sales
6		$	%
7	Department 1	$59,009	18.3%
8	Department 2	$111,601	34.6%
9	Department 3	$60,492	18.8%
10	Department 4	$68,779	21.3%
11	Department 5	$22,572	7.0%
12			
13	Total Store	$322,452	100.0%

Application Exercise 4.10 Plan Percent-to-Total and Dollar Distributions

In this exercise you will develop your own percents to plan distributions of
$175,000 for a line of designer shirts, and calculate the dollar values the per-
cents represent. This exercise will illustrate how parts, when divided, will
always equal the total.

1. Open your *Application Exercises* file.

2. Insert a blank worksheet and type and format value labels as shown in
   Figure 4.10.

3. Format cells **C12**, **C17**, **C24**, and **C29** as **currency, decimal place 0**.

4. Format cells **D12**, **D17**, **D24**, and **D29** as **percent, decimal place 1**.

5. Insert the formulas in cells **C32** and **D32** to sum the dollar and percent values that you will plan (Figure 4.10).

6. Plan percent distributions of the *total sales* by typing percent values in cells **D12**, **D17**, **D24**, and **D29**. Check cell **D32** to see that your percents total 100 percent. If they do not, adjust your percents.

7. Use formulas in cells **C12**, **C17**, **C24**, and **C29** to calculate the sales dollars that *each* designer shirt represents in the line.

   Note that the dollar value in cell **C32** equals $175,000, the total planned shirt sales.

   Note: You should recognize that each designer shirt is now a *total* that must be distributed into a style assortment.

8. Now plan percent distributions for each designer's style assortment. Enter the formulas in cells **G15**, **H15**, **G22**, **H22**, **G27**, **H27**, **G30**, **H30**, and, **G32** to sum the percent and dollar values that you will plan (Figure 4.10).

9. In cells **H12** and **H14**, plan percents of sales for style assortments of Ralph Lauren shirts. If the total in cell H15 does not equal 100 percent, adjust percents.

10. In cells **H17**, **H19**, and **H21**, plan percents to distribute sales for style assortments of Liz Claiborne shirts.

11. In cells **H24** and **H26**, plan percents to distribute sales for style assortments of Tommy Hilfiger shirts.

12. In cell **H29**, plan a percent distribution for a style assortment of Josephine Chaus shirts.

   Note that there is only one style. The *total percent* for each designer assortment should equal *100 percent*. Now use the formula to calculate the dollar distributions for items in the assortments.

   Note that *total* dollar values for each of the designer assortments is the same as the dollar values calculated for the line in cells C12, C17, C24, and C29. If your values are different, go back and check your formulas.

   Note that in cell **G32** the total for all styles in the assortments should be $175,000, which represents the total sales plan for shirts. If your value in cell **G32** is different, go back and check your formulas.

13. Rename the sheet *Percent_Dollar Plan*.

14. Save your file.

	A	B	C	D	E	F	G	H
1	*Plan Percent Distributions*							
2	*Sum of Parts = Whole*							
3	*Dollars Distribution*							
4	*Distribution Percent * Total Sales*							
5								
6			Plan the percents to total and dollar distributions for a class of shirts.					
7								
8	Total Sales for Shirts		$175,000					
9								
10	*Line*					*Assortment*		
11			$	%			$	%
12	Ralph Lauren		?	?		Long Sleeve Solids	?	?
13								
14						Long Sleeve Plaids	?	?
15						*Total*	=SUM(G12,G14)	=SUM(G12,G14)
16								
17	Liz Claiborne		?	?		Long Sleeve Solids	?	?
18								
19						Long Sleeve Plaids	?	?
20								
21						Long Sleeve Stripes	?	?
22						*Total*	=SUM(G17,G19,G21)	=SUM(H17,H19,H21)
23								
24	Tommy Hilfiger		?	?		Short Sleeve Stripes	?	?
25								
26						Short Sleeve Solids	?	?
27						*Total*	=SUM(G24,G26)	=SUM(H24,H26)
28								
29	Chaus		?	?		Short Sleeve Stripes	?	?
30						*Total*	=SUM(G29)	=SUM(H29)
31								
32	*Total*		=SUM(C12,C17,C24,C29)	=SUM(D12,D17,D24,D29)			=SUM(G15,G22,G27,G30)	

Figure 4.10 Plan percent-to-total and dollar distributions

Assignment One

In your first assignment, you will apply the Excel skills and retail-math formulas related to sales that you learned in Chapters One–Four to develop a sales plan. Go back and review the following:

▶   Formula for sales increase

▶   Formula for dollar distribution of sales

▶   Absolute reference

1.   Open your *Merchandise Budget* file that you developed in Chapter One.

2.   In cell **C4**, type **5.0** percent as the sales increase.

3.   In cell **D4**, type **$250,000** to represent last year's sales.

4. Enter a complex formula in cell **C18** to calculate a **5.0 percent** increase in last year's sales for the season/total-sales value.

5. Enter a simple formula in cell **C19** to total the monthly distribution percents that you will plan in cells **D19-I19**.

6. Plan the following distributions percents for each of the six months and type them in cells **D19:I19**:

FEB	MAR	APR	MAY	JUN	JUL
16.1%	17.3%	16.4%	17.0%	16.7%	16.5%

Note that as you insert the percents, they are totaled in cell C19. If your total is less or more than 100 percent, check to see that you entered the correct values.

7. Enter the formula with an absolute reference in Cell **D18** to calculate the dollar distribution of the season/total-sales value for **FEB.**

8. Copy the formula to other months in cells **E19:I19**.

9. Check your formulas.

10. Rename the sheet *Sales Plan*.

11. Save your file.

5 *Inventory*

Chapter Objectives

After reading this chapter, you should be able to:

▶ Explain the importance of inventory planning.

▶ Discuss the importance of stockturn.

▶ Describe methods used to plan inventory.

▶ Explain the method that should be used to plan basic inventory.

▶ Explain the method that should be used to plan fashion inventory.

▶ Explain the difference between beginning-of-month and end-of-month inventories.

▶ Use Excel and structure retail formulas to calculate:

· Stockturn
· Average inventory
· BOM inventory using the basic stock method
· BOM inventory using the percentage variation method
· BOM inventory using weeks of supply
· BOM inventory using the stock-to-sales ratio method

▶ Develop an inventory plan using previously planned sales values.

KEY TERMS

An **average inventory** is the midpoint between the highest and lowest inventory levels. Average inventory is calculated by adding the beginning inventories for each month and the ending inventory for the last month and dividing the sum by the number of months in the planning period.

Basic inventory, sometimes called *staple stock*, is inventory that is in constant demand and requires repetitive inventory levels throughout a season.

The **basic stock method** is an inventory planning method. An inventory reserve is added to the planned sales to determine the beginning-of-month inventory value.

BOM refers to the beginning-of-month inventory.

EOM refers to the end-of-month inventory.

Fashion items refers to inventory that is currently popular and in demand.

Inventory is merchandise offered for sale.

Inventory dollar plans are plans to determine and control the inventory investment required to cover planned sales.

Inventory unit plans are plans for implementing an inventory dollar plan by specifying details of the inventory purchase.

The **National Retail Federation (NRF)** is an association of retailers that provides training and advisory services to members. NRF statistics can be used as benchmarks for evaluating merchandising efforts.

Overstock refers to an excess of inventory relative to demand.

Percentage variation method is an inventory planning method based on a relationship between average sales and average inventory as determined by a stockturn goal.

SKU refers to a stock-keeping unit. Each item of inventory is assigned an alphanumeric code that identifies it based on unique characteristics including style, size, color, price, and brand. SKU is used for inventory management, identification, and tracking.

Staple stock, sometimes called basic inventory, is inventory that is in continuous demand.

Stock is used synonymously with inventory.

Stock-out refers to not having inventory to meet sales demand.

A **stock-to-sales ratio** is a measure of the level of inventory to the level of sales. It is used as an inventory planning method to achieve a balance of sales and inventory.

Stockturn, **turn**, or **turnover** refers to the number of times the average inventory is sold during a specific period.

Inventory, or **stock**, refers to products that retailers purchase from vendors to sell to customers. An adequate supply of inventory is necessary to achieve planned sales. Because inventory accounts for the largest part of retailers' liquid assets, an inventory plan is critical to financial success. Two kinds of inventory plans are required: dollar plans and unit plans. An **inventory dollar plan** specifies the amount of money to invest in inventory. The **inventory unit plan** translates the dollar plan into purchasing strategies by specifying **stock-keeping units (SKUs)**, or the number of individual items, each described according to brand, price line, style, size, and color to meet customer needs.

Retailers' major challenges are achieving inventory levels that maximize profits and avoiding **stock-out** and **overstock** conditions. Inventory stock-outs result in lower profit due to lost sales and reduced store loyalty from customer dissatisfaction. **Overstocked**, or overbought, conditions occur when there is too much inventory relative to what is required to cover sales. Investment in excess inventory ties up cash from financing, handling, storage, and insurance. Over-stocked inventory carries risks of becoming obsolete, lost, or damaged. In addition, markdowns must be taken to clear out inventory, and too many unplanned markdowns impact profit.

STOCKTURN

Inventory levels should reflect a balanced relationship between stock and sales. The most commonly used measure and target for controlling inventory is a **stockturn** rate which measures the number of times an average inventory is sold in a given time period. The more closely inventory selections match customers' needs, the faster the merchandise will sell, and the higher stockturn the retailer will achieve. Stockturn achieved on inventories can be evaluated against statistics of the **National Retail Federation**, competitors' turnover rate, and past history. Stockturn is easy to calculate and use as a guide for:

▶ Evaluating how rapidly sales are occurring

▶ Planning inventory levels

Using Stockturn to Evaluate Sales

Stockturn may be calculated in dollars or units for periods of a month, season, or year. The formula for stockturn is:

Net Sales for Period / Average Inventory for Same Period

An average inventory may be calculated for any period if beginning-of-month (BOM) and end-of-month (EOM) inventory values are available as shown below:

Month's Average Inventory = Average of 1 BOM Inventory and 1 EOM Inventory

Season's Average Inventory = Average of 6 BOMs' and Last Month's EOM

Year's Average Inventory = Average of 12 BOMs' and Last Month's EOM

Application Exercise 5.1 Calculate Stockturn

In this exercise you will use the stockturn formula to calculate stockturn for a month and a season.

1. Open your *Application Exercises* file.

2. Insert a new worksheet and type and format labels and values as shown in Figure 5.1a.

3. Format values in columns **B** and **C** as **currency, decimal place 0**.

4. Format cells **D11** and **D23** as **number, decimal place 2**.

5. Enter the formula in cell **D11** to calculate **FEB's** stockturn. Use the average function to average BOM and EOM values (Figure 5.1b).

6. Enter the formula in cell **D23** to calculate stockturn for the season. Use the average function and select the six BOM values, and while holding down the Ctrl key, select the EOM value in cell **C21** (Figure 5.1c).

7. Rename the sheet *Stockturn*.

8. Save your file.

In this application, a stockturn of 0.49 is calculated for February, which indicates that the average inventory sold less than one-half of the time during the month while the season turn was 2.81 (Figure 5.1d).

Now manipulate sales and inventory values and observe the impact on stockturn.

9. In cell **B5**, type **$196,000** to increase the season's sales. In cell **B6**, type **$38,500** to increase **FEB** sales.

Note: Because cell references were used in the formulas, the stockturn numbers are recalculated to reflect higher stockturn values for the month (1.00) and season (5.74).

Figure 5.1a

Stockturn formulas
for month and
season

	A	B	C	D	E	F
1	*Calculate Stockturn for Month and Season*					
2	*Month Stockturn = Month's Sales / Average of BOM and EOM*					
3	*Season Stockturn = Season Sales / Average of 6 BOM's and Last EOM*					
4						
5	SEASON Sales	$96,000				
6	FEB Sales	$19,000				
7						
8						
9		**BOM**	**EOM**	**Stockturn**		
10						
11	FEB	$38,000	$39,000	?		
12						
13	MAR	$39,000	$35,000			
14						
15	APR	$35,000	$31,000			
16						
17	MAY	$31,000	$33,000			
18						
19	JUN	$33,000	$29,000			
20						
21	JUL	$29,000	$34,000			
22						
23	Season			?		

Figure 5.1b

Stockturn formulas
for month and
season

	A	B	C	D	E
5	SEASON Sales	$96,000			
6	FEB Sales	**$19,000**			
7					
8					
9		**BOM**	**EOM**	**Stockturn**	
10					
11	FEB	$38,000	$39,000	=B6/AVERAGE(B11:C11)	
12					
13	MAR	$39,000	$35,000		
14					
15	APR	$35,000	$31,000		
16					
17	MAY	$31,000	$33,000		
18					
19	JUN	$33,000	$29,000		
20					
21	JUL	$29,000	$34,000		
22					
23	Season			?	

Figure 5.1c

Stockturn formulas
for month and
season

	A	B	C	D	E
5	SEASON Sales	$96,000			
6	FEB Sales	$19,000			
7					
8					
9		BOM	EOM	Stockturn	
10					
11	FEB	$38,000	$39,000	0.49	
12					
13	MAR	$39,000	$35,000		
14					
15	APR	$35,000	$31,000		
16					
17	MAY	$31,000	$33,000		
18					
19	JUN	$33,000	$29,000		
20					
21	JUL	$29,000	$34,000		
22					
23	Season			=B5/AVERAGE(B11:B21,C21)	

Figure 5.1d

Stockturn formulas
for month and
season

	A	B	C	D
5	SEASON Sales	$96,000		
6	FEB Sales	$19,000		
7				
8				
9		BOM	EOM	Stockturn
10				
11	FEB	$38,000	$39,000	0.49
12				
13	MAR	$39,000	$35,000	
14				
15	APR	$35,000	$31,000	
16				
17	MAY	$31,000	$33,000	
18				
19	JUN	$33,000	$29,000	
20				
21	JUL	$29,000	$34,000	
22				
23	Season			2.81

10. Click *undo* twice to reverse the changes.

    Now increase one of the BOM inventory values and observe the impact on stockturn levels.

11. In cell **B11**, change **FEB**'s BOM inventory to **$68,000**.

    Note: Because the average inventory values are increased but the sales values remained the same, stockturn values are reduced to .36 for FEB and to 2.50 for the season.

12. Click *undo* to reverse the change.

Using Stockturn to Plan Average Inventory and Sales Levels

Predetermined stockturn values can be used to plan average inventory levels and sales levels required to accomplish stockturn goals. If any two values are known, the stockturn formula can be transposed as follows:

Average Inventory = Sales/Stockturn

Net Sales = Average Inventory * Stockturn

Application Exercise 5.2 **Use a Stockturn Goal to Calculate an Average Inventory**

In this exercise you will use a stockturn figure to calculate average inventory.

1. Open your *Application Exercises* file.

2. Insert a blank worksheet and type labels and values as shown in Figure 5.2a.

3. Format values in cells **B6:B9** and **D6:D9** as **currency, decimal place 0**.

4. Format cells **C6:C9** as **number, decimal place 1**.

5. Enter the formula in cell **D6** to calculate the required average inventory for jackets. See Figure 5.2b.

6. Copy the formula to cells **D7:D9**. See Figure 5.2c.

7. Rename the sheet *Average Inventory*.

8. Save your file.

Now examine the impact of sales and stockturn on average inventory.

9. In cell **B6**, change the sales values to **$168,000** and note the increase in the average inventory requirement.

10. Click *undo* to reverse the change.

11. In cell **C6**, change the stockturn value to **4.0** and note the decrease in the average inventory requirement.

Figure 5.2a

Formula for
calculating the
average inventory

	A	B	C	D
1	*Calculate Average Inventory Using Stockturn Goal*			
2	*Average Inventory = Sales / Stockturn*			
3				
4				
5		Planned Season Sales	Stockturn Goal	Required Average Inventory
6	Jackets	$68,207	3.2	?
7	Skirts	$99,093	3.1	?
8	Pants	$201,618	4.0	?
9	Shirts	$60,056	2.5	?

Figure 5.2b

Formula for
calculating the
average inventory

	A	B	C	D
5		Planned Season Sales	Stockturn Goal	Required Average Inventory
6	Jackets	$68,207	3.2	=B6/C6
7	Skirts	$99,093	3.1	?
8	Pants	$201,618	4.0	?
9	Shirts	$60,056	2.5	?

Figure 5.2c

Formula for
calculating the
average inventory

	A	B	C	D
5		Planned Season Sales	Stockturn Goal	Required Average Inventory
6	Jackets	$68,207	3.2	$21,315
7	Skirts	$99,093	3.1	$31,965
8	Pants	$201,618	4.0	$50,405
9	Shirts	$60,056	2.5	$24,022

Application Exercise 5.3 Use a Stockturn Goal to Calculate Required Sales

In this exercise you will use stockturn to calculate the required sales level.

1. Open your *Application Exercises* file.

2. Insert a blank worksheet and type labels and values as shown in Figure 5.3a.

3. Format cells **B6:B9** and **D6:D9** as **currency, decimal place 0**.

4. Format cells **C6:C9** as **number, decimal place 1**.

5. Enter the formula in cell **B6** to calculate the required sales level for jackets (Figure 5.3b).

6. Copy the formula to cells **B7:B9** (Figure 5.3c).

7. Rename the sheet *Required Sales Levels*.

8. Save your file.

Now examine the impacts of stockturn and average inventory on sales.

9. In cell **C7**, change the stockturn to **3.5** and note the increase in the required sales level.

10. Click "undo" to reverse the change.

11. In cell **D7**, change the average inventory to **$30,966** and note the decrease in required sales levels.

Figure 5.3a
Formula for calculating the required sales level based on the desired stockturn

	A	B	C	D
1	**Calculate Sales Using Stockturn Goal**			
2	**Sales = Stockturn * Average Inventory**			
3				
4				
5		Required Season Sales	Stockturn Goal	Planned Average Inventory
6	Jackets	?	3.2	$21,315
7	Skirts	?	3.1	$31,966
8	Pants	?	4.0	$50,405
9	Shirts	?	2.5	$24,023

Figure 5.3b
Formula for calculating the required sales level based on the desired stockturn

	A	B	C	D
5		Required Season Sales	Stockturn Goal	Planned Average Inventory
6	Jackets	=C6*D6	3.2	$21,315
7	Skirts	?	3.1	$31,966
8	Pants	?	4.0	$50,405
9	Shirts	?	2.5	$24,023

Figure 5.3c
Formula for calculating the required sales level based on the desired stockturn

	A	B	C	D
5		Required Season Sales	Stockturn Goal	Planned Average Inventory
6	Jackets	$68,208	3.2	$21,315
7	Skirts	$99,095	3.1	$31,966
8	Pants	$201,620	4.0	$50,405
9	Shirts	$60,058	2.5	$24,023

PLANNING A BEGINNING-OF-MONTH INVENTORY

Inventory plans improve profits and clarify purchase and promotion objectives.

Retailers must have inventory to cover sales for each month in the season. At the beginning of each month, inventory must be on hand to cover sales during the month, and there must be inventory remaining at the end of each month to cover the following month's sales. There are four methods commonly used to plan beginning inventory. They are:

▶   Basic stock method

▶   Percentage variation method

▶   Weeks-of-supply method

▶   Stock-to-sales ratio method

The Basic Stock Method of Planning Inventory

The **basic stock method** is used to plan **basic** or **staple inventories** that are in constant demand and require repetitive inventory levels throughout a season.

This method provides for inventory to cover the planned sales, plus an inventory reserve. The reserve guards against stock outages of basic items in the event actual sales exceed planned sales. The primary disadvantage of this method is the investment and cost of carrying a reserve inventory if actual sales fall below those that were planned. The following formula demonstrates a season's plan for basic inventory:

Basic Stock = Season Average Inventory – Season Average Sales

BOM = Basic Stock + Planned Sales for a given time period (*week, month, season*)

Because sales of basic items are rather stable throughout a season, a stockturn goal can be estimated from the previous season with a relative degree of accuracy. The stockturn is used to calculate an **average inventory**. The basic stock method is appropriate only when the stockturn is less than the number of months in the planning period. For example, if inventory is planned for a six-month period, the stockturn should be less than six.

Application Exercise 5.4 Use the Basic Stock Method to Plan an Inventory

In this exercise you will use the basic stock formula to calculate BOM inventory. To illustrate the formula structure, each section of the formula will be developed separately. Afterwards, you will use one complex formula to calculate inventory.

1. Open your *Application Exercises* file.

2. Insert a blank worksheet and type and format labels and values as shown in Figure 5.4a.

3. Format cell **B5** as **number**, **decimal place 1**.

4. Format cell **B7** as **number**, **decimal place 0**.

5. Format cells **B6**, **B8**, **B10**, **B11**, **B12**, **B14**, and **C14** as **currency**, **decimal place 0**.

6. Enter the formula in cell **B10** to calculate the average inventory (Figure 5.4b).

7. Enter the formula in cell **B11** to calculate average sales (Figure 5.4b).

8. Enter the formula in cell **B12** to calculate the basic stock (Figure 5.4b).

9. Enter the formula in cell **B14** to add the basic stock (reserve) to FEB sales (Figure 5.4c).

10. Rename the sheet *Basic Stock Inventory*.

11. Save your file.

12. In cell **C14**, observe Excel's order of operations, and structure one complex formula to calculate FEB BOM inventory (Figure 5.4c).

    Note that the BOM value is the same as that calculated in several steps (Figure 5.4d).

13. Save your file.

Now examine the impacts of stockturn and average inventory on FEB planned BOM inventory.

14. In cell **B5**, change the stockturn goal to **6**.

    Note that the basic stock is recalculated to zero because the average inventory is recalculated to $25,000, the *same* as average sales. As a result, the BOM inventory does not have a reserve and is the same as FEB planned sales. The basic stock method of inventory requires that stockturn be less than the number of months in the season.

The Percentage Variation Method of Planning Inventory

The **percentage variation method** of inventory planning correlates monthly inventory levels with variations in monthly sales. This method is best used for **fashion items** or inventory with a high turnover of three or more times

Figure 5.4a
Formula for basic
stock inventory
planning method

	A	B	C	D	E
1	*Calculate BOM Inventory with Basic Stock Method*				
2	*Basic Stock = Season Average Inventory - Season Average Sales*				
3	*Planned BOM Inventory = Basic Stock + Month's Planned Sales*				
4					
5	Stockturn Goal	3.2			
6	Season's Planned sales	$150,000			
7	Number of Months in Season	6			
8	FEB. Planned Sales	$21,652			
9					
10	Season Average Inventory	?			
11	Season Average Sales	?			
12	Basic Stock	?			
13					
14	FEB. Planned BOM Inventory	?	?		

Figure 5.4b
Formula for basic
stock inventory
planning method

	A	B	C	D	E
5	Stockturn Goal	3.2			
6	Season's Planned sales	$150,000			
7	Number of Months in Season	6			
8	FEB. Planned Sales	$21,652			
9					
10	Season Average Inventory	=B6/B5			
11	Season Average Sales	=B6/B7			
12	Basic Stock	=B10-B11			
13					
14	FEB. Planned BOM Inventory	?	?		

Figure 5.4c
Formula for basic
stock inventory
planning method

	A	B	C	D	E
5	Stockturn Goal	3.2			
6	Season's Planned sales	$150,000			
7	Number of Months in Season	6			
8	FEB. Planned Sales	$21,652			
9					
10	Season Average Inventory	$46,875			
11	Season Average Sales	$25,000			
12	Basic Stock	$21,875			
13					
14	FEB. Planned BOM Inventory	=B8+B12	=(B6/B5)-(B6/B7)+B8		

Figure 5.4d

Formula for basic
stock inventory
planning method

	A	B	C	D	E
5	Stockturn Goal	3.2			
6	Season's Planned sales	$150,000			
7	Number of Months in Season	6			
8	FEB. Planned Sales	$21,652			
9					
10	Season Average Inventory	**$46,875**			
11	Season Average Sales	**$25,000**			
12	Basic Stock	**$21,875**			
13					
14	**FEB. Planned BOM Inventory**	**$43,527**	**$43,527**		

per season. Unlike the basic stock method, there is no consistent reserve each month. Because fashion items do not have a predictable product life, inventory reserves are not required. Percentage variation is based on the premise that BOM inventory is increased or decreased from the planned average inventory by half of the percentage that planned monthly sales vary from the average monthly sales.

The formula for percentage variation is as follows:

$$\text{BOM} = \text{Average Inventory} * .50 \left(\frac{1+ \text{Month's Planned Sales}}{\text{Planned Average Monthly Sales}} \right)$$

$$\text{Average Inventory} = \frac{\text{Planned Season Sales}}{\text{Stockturn}}$$

Application Exercise 5.5 Use the Percentage Variation Method to Plan an Inventory

In this exercise you will use the percentage variation method to calculate a BOM inventory for one month in a six-month season. To illustrate the formula structure, each section of the formula will be developed separately. Afterwards, you will use one complex formula to calculate inventory.

1. Open your *Application Exercises* file.

2. Insert a blank worksheet and type and format labels and values as shown in Figure 5.5a.

3. Format cell **B5** as **number, decimal place 1**.

4. Format cell **B7** as **number, decimal place 0**.

5. Format cells **B10, B13, B15**, and **C15** as **currency, decimal place 0**.

6. Format cells **B11** and **B12** as **percent, decimal place 1**.

7. In cell **B10**, enter the formula to calculate average sales (Figure 5.5b).

8. In cell **B13**, enter the formula to calculate the average inventory (Figure 5.5b).

9. In cell **B11**, enter the formula to calculate the percentage of planned sales to average sales (Figure 5.5c).

10. In cell **B12**, enter the formula to calculate half of the variation (Figure 5.5c).

11. In cell **B15**, enter the formula to calculate FEB's BOM inventory (Figure 5.5c).

    Note: Planned sales are 86.6% of average sales. The difference between 86.6% and 100% is 13.4%. One-half of 13.4 is 6.7%. This percent, 6.7%, represents the percent that the BOM should vary from the average inventory. The difference between 6.7% and 100 is 93.3%.

12. Rename the sheet *Percentage Variation*.

13. Save your file.

14. In cell **C15**, observe the order operations and structure one complex formula to calculate FEB's BOM inventory (Figure 5.5c).

    Note that the BOM is the same as that calculated in several steps (Figure 5.5d).

15. Save your file.

Now examine the impact of FEB's planned sales on FEB's planned BOM inventory.

16. In cell **B8**, change FEB's planned sales to **$15,000**.

    Note that when FEB sales are decreased, the BOM inventory is also decreased.

Figure 5.5a

Formula for percentage variation inventory planning Method

	A	B	C	D	E	F
1	*Calculate BOM Inventory with Percentage Variation Method*					
2	*BOM = Average Inventory * .50 (1+ Month's Planned Sales / Average Monthly Sales)*					
3						
4						
5	Stockturn Goal	3.2				
6	Season's Planned Sales	$150,000				
7	Number of Months in Season	6				
8	FEB. Planned Sales	$21,652				
9						
10	Average Sales	?				
11	Percent of Planned Sales to Average Sales	?				
12	One Half of Percent Variation	?				
13	Average Inventory	?				
14						
15	FEB. BOM Inventory	?	?			

Figure 5.5b
Formula for
percentage variation
inventory planning
method

	A	B	C	D	E	F
5	Stockturn Goal	3.2				
6	Season's Planned Sales	$150,000				
7	Number of Months in Season	6				
8	FEB. Planned Sales	$21,652				
9						
10	Average Sales	=B6/B7				
11	Percent of Planned Sales to Average Sales	?				
12	One Half of Percent Variation	?				
13	Average Inventory	=B6/B5				
14						
15	FEB. BOM Inventory	?	?			

Figure 5.5c
Formula for
percentage variation
inventory planning
method

	A	B	C	D	E	F
5	Stockturn Goal	3.2				
6	Season's Planned Sales	$150,000				
7	Number of Months in Season	6				
8	FEB. Planned Sales	$21,652				
9						
10	Average Sales	$25,000				
11	Percent of Planned Sales to Average Sales	=B8/B10				
12	One Half of Percent Variation	=0.5*(1+B11)				
13	Average Inventory	$46,875				
14						
15	FEB. BOM Inventory	=B12*B13	=(B6/B5)*0.5*(1+(B8/B10))			

Figure 5.5d
Formula for
percentage variation
inventory planning
method

	A	B	C	D	E	F
5	Stockturn Goal	3.2				
6	Season's Planned Sales	$150,000				
7	Number of Months in Season	6				
8	FEB. Planned Sales	$21,652				
9						
10	Average Sales	$25,000				
11	Percent of Planned Sales to Average Sales	86.6%				
12	One Half of Percent Variation	93.3%				
13	Average Inventory	$46,875				
14						
15	FEB. BOM Inventory	$43,736	$43,736			

The Weeks-of-Supply Method of Planning Inventory

Weeks-of-supply is an inventory planning method for planning inventory
that does not fluctuate in sales volume from week to week. With this method,
the supply of basic inventory that is kept on hand is dependent on the desired
stockturn for a planning period. The weeks-of-supply method plans BOM

levels in direct proportion to planned average sales. This means that during weeks when sales and stockturn are above or below average, inventory levels will be inadequate. The stockturn number is used to calculate the supply of inventory required for a predetermined number of weeks. The formula for weeks of supply is:

$$BOM = \text{Average Weekly Sales} * \text{Number of Weeks of Supply}$$

$$\text{Number of Weeks of Supply} = \frac{\text{Number of Weeks in Period}}{\text{Planned Stockturn for Period}}$$

Application Exercise 5.6 Use the Weeks-of-Supply Method to Plan an Inventory

In this exercise you will use the weeks-of-supply method to calculate a BOM for a six-month season. To illustrate the formula structure, each section of the formula will be developed separately. Afterwards, you will use one complex formula to calculate the inventory.

1. Open your *Application Exercises* file.

2. Insert a blank worksheet and type and format labels and values as shown in Figure 5.6a.

3. Format cells **B5** and **B11** as **number, decimal place 1**.

4. Format cell **B7** as **number, decimal place 0**.

5. Format cells **B10**, **B13**, and **C13** as **currency, decimal place 0**.

6. Enter the formula in cell **B10** to calculate average weekly sales (Figure 5.6b).

7. Enter the formula in cell **B11** to calculate the number of weeks of supply (Figure 5.6b).

8. In cell **B13**, enter the formula to calculate BOM for FEB (Figure 5.6b).

9. Rename the sheet *Weeks of Supply*.

10. Save your file.

11. In cell **C13**, observe the order operations and structure one complex formula to calculate FEB's BOM inventory (Figure 5.6c).

    Note that the BOM inventory value is the same as that calculated in several steps (Figure 5.6d).

    A beginning inventory of $46,875 calculated in this application means that if sales remain average, at the end of every eight weeks, inventory will

Figure 5.6a

Formula for weeks-of-supply inventory planning method

	A	B	C	D	E	F
1	*Calculate BOM Inventory with Weeks Supply Method*					
2	*BOM = Average Weekly Sales * Number of Weeks of Supply*					
3	*Number of Weeks of Supply = Number of Weeks in Period / Stockturn Goal*					
4						
5	Stockturn Goal	3.2				
6	Season's Planned Sales	$150,000				
7	Number of Weeks in Season	26				
8						
9						
10	Average Weekly Sales	?				
11	Number of Weeks of Supply	?				
12						
13	FEB. BOM Inventory	?	?			

Figure 5.6b

Formula for weeks-of-supply inventory planning method

	A	B	C
5	Stockturn Goal	3.2	
6	Season's Planned Sales	$150,000	
7	Number of Weeks in Season	26	
8			
9			
10	Average Weekly Sales	=B6/B7	
11	Number of Weeks of Supply	=B7/B5	
12			
13	FEB. BOM Inventory	=B10*B11	?

Figure 5.6c

Formula for weeks-of-supply inventory planning method

	A	B	C	
5	Stockturn Goal	3.2		
6	Season's Planned Sales	$150,000		
7	Number of Weeks in Season	26		
8				
9				
10	Average Weekly Sales	**$5,769**		
11	Number of Weeks of Supply	8.1		
12				
13	FEB. BOM Inventory	**$46,875**	=(B6/B7)*(B7/B5)	

Figure 5.6d

Formula for weeks-
of-supply inventory
planning method

	A	B	C
5	Stockturn Goal	3.2	
6	Season's Planned Sales	$150,000	
7	Number of Weeks in Season	26	
8			
9			
10	Average Weekly Sales	**$5,769**	
11	Number of Weeks of Supply	8.1	
12			
13	**FEB. BOM Inventory**	**$46,875**	**$46,875**

be depleted. This allows inventory to be reordered on a weekly or biweekly basis.

Now examine the impacts of stockturn and average inventory on FEB's BOM.

12.   In cell **B5**, change the stockturn goal to **5**.

Note that when the stockturn goal is increased, the supply of inventory required, as well as the number of weeks to stock, is decreased.

The Stock-to-Sales Ratio Method of Planning Inventory

The **stock to sales** ratio is a method of evaluating and planning inventory based on an assumption that the retailer should maintain a certain ratio of inventory to sales. Ratios can be based on National Retail Federation statistics, store or department policy, or historical data. Stock to sales ratios vary among products, time periods, departments, and retailers. Sales and inventory values for the same period are required to calculate stock sales ratios. The period may be weeks, months, or any selling period for which data are available. The ratio can be expressed as a whole number or fraction.

A stock to sales ratio may be used to plan either BOM or EOM inventory values. The choice between BOM and EOM is influenced by a retailer's accounting practices and available data.

The formulas for stock to sales ratio and calculating BOM using stock to sales ratio are:

$$\text{Stock to Sales Ratio} = \frac{\text{Inventory}}{\text{Sales}}$$

$$\text{BOM Inventory} = \text{Stock to Sales Ratio} * \text{Planned Sales}$$

In this exercise you will use the stock-to-sales ratio method to calculate inventory. The ratios will be calculated from last season's sales and inventory values. The ratios will then be used to calculate BOMs for a six-month period.

1.   Open your *Application Exercises* file.

2.   Insert a blank worksheet and type and format labels and values as shown in Figure 5.7a.

3.   Format cells **C8:H8** as **number, decimal place 1**.

4.   Format cells **C13:H13** as **currency, decimal place 0**.

5.   Enter the formula in cell **C8** to calculate last season's stock-to-sales ratio (Figure 5.7b).

6.   Copy the formula to cells **D8:H8**.

7.   Enter the formula in cell **C13** to calculate the planned BOM inventory (Figure 5.7c).

8.   Copy the formula to cells **D13:H13** (Figure 5.7c).

9.   Rename the sheet *Stock Sales Ratio*.

10. Save your file.

11. Now examine the impact that last season's inventory and planned sales have on the ratio and planned BOM. In cell **C6**, increase last season's

	A	B	C	D	E	F	G	H
1	*Calculate BOM Inventory with Stock to Sales Ratio Method*							
2	*Stock to Sales Ratio = Inventory / Sales*							
3	*BOM = Planned Sales * Stock/Sales Ratio*							
4								
5			FEB	MAR	APR	MAY	JUN	JUL
6	Last Season Sales		$17,890	$17,360	$18,763	$17,692	$17,210	$17,631
7	Last Season BOM Inventory		$46,514	$36,456	$45,219	$40,869	$38,206	$37,907
8	Last Season Stock/Sales Ratio		?	?	?	?	?	?
9								
10								
11	Planned Sales		$19,679	$19,096	$20,639	$19,461	$18,931	$19,394
12	Planned Stock/Sales Ratio							
13	Planned BOM Inventory		?	?	?	?	?	?

Figure 5.7a Formula for stock-to-sales ratio inventory planning method

	A	B	C	D	E	F	G	H
5			FEB	MAR	APR	MAY	JUN	JUL
6	Last Season Sales		$17,890	$17,360	$18,763	$17,692	$17,210	$17,631
7	Last Season BOM Inventory		$46,514	$36,456	$45,219	$40,869	$38,206	$37,907
8	Last Season Stock/Sales Ratio		=C7/C6	?	?	?	?	?
9								
10								
11	Planned Sales		$19,679	$19,096	$20,639	$19,461	$18,931	$19,394
12	Planned Stock/Sales Ratio							
13	Planned BOM Inventory		=C11*C8	?	?	?	?	?

Figure 5.7b Formula for stock-to-sales ratio inventory planning method

	A	B	C	D	E	F	G	H
5			FEB	MAR	APR	MAY	JUN	JUL
6	Last Season Sales		$17,890	$17,360	$18,763	$17,692	$17,210	$17,631
7	Last Season BOM Inventory		$46,514	$36,456	$45,219	$40,869	$38,206	$37,907
8	Last Season Stock/Sales Ratio		2.6	2.1	2.4	2.3	2.2	2.2
9								
10								
11	Planned Sales		$19,679	$19,096	$20,639	$19,461	$18,931	$19,394
12	Planned Stock/Sales Ratio		2.6	2.1	2.4	2.3	2.2	2.2
13	Planned BOM Inventory		$51,165	$40,102	$49,741	$44,955	$42,027	$41,697

Figure 5.7c Formula for stock-to-sales ratio inventory planning method

FEB sales to **$25,000**. Note that the ratio decreases as does the planned BOM for FEB.

12. In Cell **C7**, increase last season's FEB inventory to **$60,000**. Note that the ratio increases as does the planned BOM for FEB.

END-OF-MONTH INVENTORIES

The four inventory planning methods are used to plan the beginning-of-month inventory level to ensure that inventory will be available to cover sales during a given month. End-of-month inventory levels must be considered because merchandise needs to be available at the end of each month to carry over and cover sales for the next month. EOM inventory values do not have to be calculated because the closing inventory for one month becomes the

	A	B	C	D	E	F	G	H
1	*Plan Ending Inventory*							
2		*EOM = Next Month's BOM*						
3								
4								
5			FEB	MAR	APR	MAY	JUN	JUL
6	Planned sales		$19,679	$19,096	$20,639	$19,461	$18,931	$19,394
7								
8	Planned BOM		$51,165	$40,101	$49,740	$44,955	$42,026	$41,697
9	Planned EOM		=D8	=E8	=F8	=G8	=H8	=AVERAGE(C8:H8)

Figure 5.8a Ending inventory values referenced from BOM values

	A	B	C	D	E	F	G	H
5			FEB	MAR	APR	MAY	JUN	JUL
6	Planned sales		$19,679	$19,096	$20,639	$19,461	$18,931	$19,394
7								
8	Planned BOM		$51,165	$40,101	$49,740	$44,955	$42,026	$41,697
9	Planned EOM		**$40,101**	**$49,740**	**$44,955**	**$42,026**	**$41,697**	**$44,947**

Figure 5.8b Ending inventory values referenced from BOM values

opening inventory for the next month. Therefore, the BOM calculated for one month represents the EOM for the previous month (Figure 5.8b). When developing an inventory plan for a six-month period, the ending inventory value for the last month in the season can be estimated as an average of the six BOM values. See the formula in Figure 5.8a.

Assignment Two

For your second assignment you will apply the Excel skills and retail-math formulas related to inventory that you learned in Chapters One–Five to develop an inventory plan based on sales that were planned in Assignment One. You will use functions, cell references, and absolute references in your formulas to calculate inventory with the percentage variation method.

1. Open your *Merchandise Budget* file.

2. Check your sales plan and correct any formula errors.

3. Create a copy of your *Sales Plan* sheet and rename the copy *Inventory Plan*. Position the *inventory* sheet after the *sales* sheet.

4. Insert a season stock turnover goal of **3.5** in cell **C13**.

5. Enter one complex formula in cell **D21** to calculate FEB's BOM using the **percentage variation method**.

   Note: Use the season's planned stockturn in cell **C13** in the formula to calculate the average inventory. Use absolute references so the formula can be copied to other months.

   Hint: The FEB BOM value should be **$73,725**. If yours is different, go back and check your formula.

6. Use the fill handle and copy the formula to Cells **E21:I21**.

7. In cell **C21**, use the formula to reference FEB's BOM as the season's opening inventory.

8. In cell **D23**, use a formula to reference MAR's BOM as FEB's EOM. Copy the formula to cells **E23:H23**.

9. In cell **I23**, enter the formula to average FEB through JUL's BOM values.

   Note: Because you are planning inventory, the average of the monthly BOM values will be used as an estimate of the season's ending inventory.

10. In cell **C23**, use the formula to reference JUL's EOM as the season's ending inventory.

11. In cell **D22**, enter the formula to calculate the stock-to-sales ratio for FEB. Copy the formula to the other months. Do not calculate a total stock-to-sales ratio.

12. Calculate the season's average inventory in cell **C41**.

    Note that you must use FEB-through-JUL BOM values and JUL's EOM in your formula.

13. Calculate each month's average inventory. In cell **C41**, enter the formula to calculate average inventory. Copy the formula to the other months.

14. Calculate monthly stockturn values. Use the Season/Total sales and average inventory values and enter the formula in cell **C43** to calculate stockturn for the season. Copy the formula to the months.

15. Save your file.

6 *Planning Reductions*

Chapter Objectives

After reading this chapter you should be able to:

- ▶ Define reductions.
- ▶ Explain the importance of reductions planning.
- ▶ Discuss reasons for markdown and sales discounts.
- ▶ Explain causes of inventory shrinkage.
- ▶ Differentiate between the types of markdowns.
- ▶ Explain different ways in which markdown percent is calculated.
- ▶ Explain the importance of sell-through analysis.
- ▶ Demonstrate steps in planning reductions.
- ▶ Use Excel and structure retail formulas to calculate:
  - · Markdown dollars
  - · Markdown percent
  - · Sales-discount dollars
  - · Sales-discount percent
  - · Shrinkage dollars
  - · Shrinkage percent
  - · Sell through
- ▶ Develop a reductions plan using previously planned sales and inventory values.

KEY TERMS

Automatic markdowns are the lowering of retail prices by fixed percentages on a predetermined time schedule.

Average unit retail prices (AUR) are the average prices at which items or units in an inventory are sold.

Markdown cancellations are upward revisions of prices that were previously reduced by markdown. A markdown cancellation returns merchandise to its premarkdown price.

Markdowns are the most common price adjustments that result in the lowering of the current retail price.

Permanent markdowns are price reductions taken for the purpose of clearing out old inventory.

Promotional markdowns are reductions in retail prices for the purpose of stimulating customer interest. A promotional markdown is canceled after a specific period.

Reductions are the sum total of markdowns, employee sales discounts, and shrinkage. Reductions decrease the retail value of inventory.

Sales discounts are price adjustments to a lower retail price for store employees and sometimes customers who fall into special categories.

Seasonal markdowns are price reductions at the end of a prime selling season.

A **sell through** is an inventory evaluation technique that reflects the percentage of beginning on-hand or original inventory sold during a specific time. Also called *sell-thru*.

Shortage or **shrinkage** is a reduction in inventory resulting from theft and errors in recording and tracking inventory. Shrinkage is determined by comparing the book-value of inventory with a physical count of inventory items.

Stagger markdowns are a method of liquidating inventory through price adjustments whereby inventory is marked down in stages.

After sales and inventory planning, the next stage in the planning process is the development of a reductions plan. **Reductions** are made up of markdowns, employee sales discounts, and shrinkage. Reductions decrease the retail value of inventory because they impact the inventory that is available for sale and are significant factors in determining the price of merchandise. Markdowns and sales discounts are desirable reductions because they serve specific purposes for retailers. For example, markdowns are used to clear out inventory and increase stockturn, and employee sales discounts are used as incentives for current and prospective employees. On the other hand, shrinkage or *shortage* is a kind of reduction that must be planned for to diminish the negative impact of theft or errors in accounting of inventory.

MARKDOWNS

A **markdown** is a price adjustment that results in the reduction of a product's selling price. Markdowns comprise the largest portion of retailers' reductions. Although markdowns lower a retailer's profit margin, they are important for improving sales, stock turnover, and store patronage. Markdowns are classified as promotional or permanent, both of which are used to generate higher profits, increase store traffic, and address errors related to buying and pricing. For example, economic conditions or a competitor's actions may reduce consumer traffic, and markdowns are required to attract customers into the store and to meet competitive prices. Mistakes in buying the wrong merchandise, buying too many units, and inventory that is damaged or soiled require price reductions to clear out inventory.

Promotional Markdowns

A **promotional markdown** is the most common method for stimulating customer interest using price. A product is offered for sale at a promotional price that is lower than the normal selling price with the purpose of introducing the product and encouraging purchase. With a promotional markdown, the lowered price is for only a specific period of time and is recorded at the time of sale.

With promotional markdowns the price tags on items stay the same and the markdown is taken at the register when the sale is rung up. For example, promotional markdowns may be taken on coats for a preseason sale. At the end of the promotional period, the merchandise is returned to its premarkdown retail price through **markdown cancellation**, and coats are sold at the higher retail price until midseason, when permanent markdowns may be taken.

Permanent Markdowns

A **permanent markdown** is taken for the purpose of clearing out old inventory. The goal of permanent markdowns is to keep inventory fresh. If inventory is not selling, permanent markdowns are used to free up space occupied by obsolete or discontinued inventory so it can be replaced with new, faster-turning merchandise. The timing for permanent markdowns is influenced by the type of product, the season, and store policy. Merchandise-return policy may be prohibited or limited for products purchased with permanent markdowns.

Seasonal Markdowns

Retailers of seasonal merchandise such as clothing, gardening products, sporting goods, and holiday items must sell a fixed inventory over a short selling season. Because of the difficulty in predicting demand for fashion and style from one season to the next, retailers offer price reductions at the end of the prime selling season to clear out seasonal inventory. Success in determining what items to markdown, the point in the season to begin markdowns, and the markdown amount can mean the difference between profit and loss for retailers of seasonal inventory.

The Timing and Size of Markdowns

The use of markdowns reflects a store's image and is dictated by a retailer's pricing policy. The timing of markdowns can mean the difference between large losses and modest profits. For example, markdowns taken early in the season when sales are declining but product interest is still relatively high will require lower markdowns. Early markdowns will generate inventory dollars and free up floor space for new purchases by clearing out slow-moving items. Conversely, markdowns taken later in the season provide a wider window of opportunity to sell inventory at its original price, but will require a larger markdown to stimulate sales at the end of a season. Some retailers **stagger markdowns** throughout the season by progressively liquidating existing stock through markdowns in different stages. Other retailers employ an **automatic markdown** policy to reduce prices by fixed percentages on a predetermined time schedule.

Calculating Markdown Dollars

Markdown is a price adjustment that reflects the dollar difference between the original retail price and the new retail price. The formula for dollar markdown on an individual item is:

Dollar Markdown = Original Retail Price – New Retail Price

In an inventory consisting of multiple items of varying unit prices, the same formula is used. However, to determine the total markdown for the entire inventory, dollar markdown must be calculated for each item and multiplied by the number of units to determine total markdown cost, as illustrated with the following formula:

Total-Dollar Markdown = (Original Retail Price – New Retail Price) * Number of Units

Application Exercise 6.1 Use Formulas to Calculate a Total-Dollar Markdown

You will use the markdown formula to calculate a total-dollar markdown for a group of items consisting of various units and prices.

1. Open your *Application Exercises* file.

2. Insert a blank worksheet and type and format the values and labels as shown in Figure 6.1a.

3. Format cell range **E7:F10** as **currency**, **decimal place 0**.

4. Enter the formula in cell **E7** to calculate individual markdown dollars for jackets (Figure 6.1b). Copy the formula to **E8:E9**.

5. Enter the formula in cell **F7** to calculate the total markdown for ten units of jackets (Figure 6.1b). Copy the formulas to **F8:F9**.

6. Enter the formula in cell **F10** to sum markdown dollars for inventory (Figure 6.1c).

7. Rename the sheet *Calculate Markdown*.

8. Save your file.

	A	B	C	D	E	F	G	H
1	*Calculate Markdown Dollars on Inventory*							
2	*Markdown Dollars on Inventory = (Original Retail Price - New Retail Price) * Units*							
3								
4								
5		# Units	Original	New	Individual	Total		
6			Retail	Retail	Markdown	Markdown		
7	Jackets	10	$128	$97	?	?		
8	Skirts	25	$89	$75	?	?		
9	Blouses	18	$48	$35	?	?		
10	*Total*					?		

Figure 6.1a Formulas for calculating markdown dollars on inventory

Figure 6.1b

Formulas for
calculating
markdown dollars
on inventory

	A	B	C	D	E	F
5		# Units	Original	New	Individual	Total
6			Retail	Retail	Markdown	Markdown
7	Jackets	10	$128	$97	=C7-D7	=E7*B7
8	Skirts	25	$89	$75	?	?
9	Blouses	18	$48	$35	?	?
10	*Total*					?

Figure 6.1c

Formulas for
calculating
markdown dollars
on inventory

	A	B	C	D	E	F
5		# Units	Original	New	Individual	Total
6			Retail	Retail	Markdown	Markdown
7	Jackets	10	$128	$97	$31	$310
8	Skirts	25	$89	$75	$14	$350
9	Blouses	18	$48	$35	$13	$234
10	*Total*					=SUM(F7:F9)

Calculating Markdown as a Percent Off Retail Price

Markdown is expressed as a percent. The markdown percent that retailers advertise to consumers is one that must encourage them to buy. Because consumers are interested in the difference between the original price and the new price, markdown is expressed as a percent off the original price. The formula is as follows:

$$\text{Off-Retail Markdown Percent} = \frac{\text{Original Retail Price} - \text{New Retail Price}}{\text{Original Retail Price}}$$

Application Exercise 6.2 Use Formulas to Calculate a Markdown's Off-Retail Percent

In this exercise you will use the markdown percent formula to calculate markdown as a percent off original retail.

1. Open your *Application Exercises* file.

2. Make a copy of your *Calculate Markdown* sheet.

3. Rename the copied sheet *Markdown Percent*.

4. Add labels to columns **G** and **H** as shown in Figure 6.2a.

5. Format cells **G7:G10** as **currency, decimal place 0**.

6. Format cells **H7:H10** as **percent, decimal place 1**.

7. Enter the formula in cell **G7** to calculate the original retail price for ten units of jackets. Copy the formula to **G8:G9** (Figure 6.2b).

8. Enter the formula in cell **G10** to sum total original retail for the inventory (Figure 6.2b).

9. Enter the formula in cell **H7** to calculate the markdown percent off original retail for jackets. Copy the formula to **H8:H10** (Figures 6.2c and 6.2d).

	A	B	C	D	E	F	G	H	I
1	*Calculate Markdown Percent on Inventory*								
2	*Markdown Percent on Inventory = Total Markdown Dollars / Total Original Retail Dollars*								
3									
4									
5		# Units	Original	New	Individual	Total	Total	Markdown	
6			Retail	Retail	Markdown	Markdown	Original Retail	Percent	
7	Jackets	10	$128	$97	$31	$310	?	?	
8	Skirts	25	$89	$75	$14	$350	?	?	
9	Blouses	18	$48	$35	$13	$234	?	?	
10	*Total*					$894	?	?	

Figure 6.2a Formula for calculating markdown as a percent off original retail

	A	B	C	D	E	F	G	H
5		# Units	Original	New	Individual	Total	Total	Markdown
6			Retail	Retail	Markdown	Markdown	Original Retail	Percent
7	Jackets	10	$128	$97	$31	$310	=C7*B7	?
8	Skirts	25	$89	$75	$14	$350	=C8*B8	?
9	Blouses	18	$48	$35	$13	$234	=C9*B9	?
10	*Total*					$894	=SUM(G7:G9)	?

Figure 6.2b Formula for calculating markdown as a percent off original retail

	A	B	C	D	E	F	G	H
5		# Units	Original	New	Individual	Total	Total	Markdown
6			Retail	Retail	Markdown	Markdown	Original Retail	Percent
7	Jackets	10	$128	$97	$31	$310	$1,280	=F7/G7
8	Skirts	25	$89	$75	$14	$350	$2,225	=F8/G8
9	Blouses	18	$48	$35	$13	$234	$864	=F9/G9
10	*Total*					$894	$4,369	=F10/G10

Figure 6.2c Formula for calculating markdown as a percent off original retail

	A	B	C	D	E	F	G	H
5		# Units	Original Retail	New Retail	Individual Markdown	Total Markdown	Total Original Retail	Markdown Percent
6								
7	Jackets	10	$128	$97	$31	$310	$1,280	24.2%
8	Skirts	25	$89	$75	$14	$350	$2,225	15.7%
9	Blouses	18	$48	$35	$13	$234	$864	27.1%
10	*Total*					$894	$4,369	67.0%

Figure 6.2d Formula for calculating markdown as a percent off original retail

10. Save your file.

Note that the total markdown percent is different from markdown percents for individual items in the inventory because of variations in the number of units and unit prices (Figure 6.2d).

Calculating Markdown as a Percent of Net Sales

Retailers' expression of markdowns reflects the cost of markdowns or the dollars lost from taking a markdown on an inventory. Dollar markdown is calculated as the difference between the original value of the inventory and the value of the inventory when sold. The difference is expressed as a percent of the net sales. The formula is as follows:

$$\text{Markdown Percent of Sales} = \frac{\text{Dollar Markdown}}{\text{Net Sales}}$$

Last season's markdown value can be used as the starting point when planning a markdown as a total percent of sales. This percent can be adjusted and used to plan the total-dollar markdown for a future season. The season's total-dollar markdown is calculated with the following formula:

Season's Dollar Markdown = Planned Markdown Percent * Planned Sales

A season's total-dollar markdown must be distributed among the months in the season. Markdown distributions are planned as percents of the total markdown value. Because the season's total markdown value represents 100 percent, the distribution percents when added, must equal 100 percent. As with sales planning, last season's distribution percents are the starting point for planning estimates. The dollar-distribution formula used to calculate months' dollar markdown is as follows:

Month's Dollar Markdown =
Total Dollar Markdown * Month's Planned Distribution Percent

Application Exercise 6.3 Use Formulas to Calculate a Season's Dollar Markdown

In this exercise, last year (LY) will be used to plan a markdown. LY's markdown percent will be calculated first. Afterwards, it will be used to calculate the total markdown dollars for the next season.

1. Open your *Application Exercises* file.

2. Insert a blank worksheet and type and format the values and labels as shown in Figure 6.3a.

3. Format cell **C7** as **percent, decimal place 1**.

4. Format cells **C5, C6, C9,** and **C10** as **currency, decimal place 0**.

5. Enter the formula in cell **C7** to calculate LY's markdown percent (Figure 6.3b).

Figure 6.3a
Formulas for markdown percent and markdown dollars

	A	B	C	D	E
1	*Plan Markdown Dollars Using LY Values*				
2	*Markdown Percent = Markdown Dollars / Net Sales*				
3	*Markdown Dollars = Markdown Percent * Planned Sales*				
4					
5	LY Net Sales		$150,700		
6	LY Markdown		$25,631		
7	LY Markdown Percent for Season		?		
8					
9	Planned Sales- Fall 2010		$162,048		
10	Planned Markdown - Fall 2010		?		

Figure 6.3b
Formulas for markdown percent and markdown dollars

	A	B	C
5	LY Net Sales		$150,700
6	LY Markdown		$25,631
7	LY Markdown Percent for Season		=C6/C5
8			
9	Planned Sales- Fall 2010		$162,048
10	Planned Markdown - Fall 2010		?

Figure 6.3c
Formulas for
markdown percent
and markdown
dollars

	A	B	C
5	LY Net Sales		$150,700
6	LY Markdown		$25,631
7	LY Markdown Percent for Season		17.0%
8			
9	Planned Sales- Fall 2010		$162,048
10	Planned Markdown - Fall 2010		=C7*C9

Figure 6.3d
Formulas for
markdown percent
and markdown
dollars

	A	B	C
5	LY Net Sales		$150,700
6	LY Markdown		$25,631
7	LY Markdown Percent for Season		17.0%
8			
9	Planned Sales- Fall 2010		$162,048
10	Planned Markdown - Fall 2010		$27,561

6. Enter the formula in cell **C10** to calculate Fall 2010's total-dollar markdown (Figure 6.3c and d).

7. Rename the sheet *Calculate Markdown*.

8. Save your file.

Markdowns and Sell-through Analysis

Markdowns are usually planned for the season. However, there are situations during a season when unplanned markdowns may be necessary. Unplanned markdowns may occur as a result of sell-through analysis. **Sell-through** analysis is an inventory evaluation technique used to determine the percentage of beginning on-hand inventory sold within a specific time period—most commonly a month or season. Sell through is used most often to analyze results in seasonal departments or promotions. For both retailers and manufacturers, high sell-through percents are desirable. A low sell through signals poor sales or too much inventory. Sell through is important because it identifies inventory items that are fast-sellers or slow-movers and facilitates markdown, transfer, return-to-vendor, and reorder decisions. For manufacturers, the development of promotions and special advertising may be required to increase the sell-through rate of their products. For retailers, sell-through evaluation provides early and continuing direction relative to what products should be marked down or reordered. Retailers may establish different benchmark sell-through percents for different categories in their inventories to determine which items to mark down. If low sell-through percents are identified, markdowns can be taken early in the season and will be less costly than if taken later.

Inventory assortment and seasonality influence sell through. For example, sell through for inventory with a wide range of SKUs will be higher at the beginning of a season, when the full-range assortment of sizes and colors are available for purchase. As styles, colors, and size selections are reduced, the sell-through percent will be reduced. Sell through for seasonal inventory will be higher during peak season and lower at season's end, when interest and need for seasonal products diminish.

Sell-through percents are normally calculated with inventory units. However, as long as the same measurements are used in the formula, inventory dollar values can also be used. The following formulas are used to calculate sell through using unit and dollar values, respectively:

$$\text{Sell-through Percent} = \frac{\text{Number of Units Sold}}{(\text{Number of Units on-Hand} + \text{Number of Units Sold})}$$

$$\text{Sell-through Percent} = \frac{\text{Sales}}{(\text{Dollar Value of Units on Hand} + \text{Sales})}$$

If sell through is calculated with unit dollar values, the **average unit retail price** may be required to convert units sold to sales as shown in the following formula:

$$\text{Sales Dollars} = \text{Units Sold} * \text{Average Unit Retail Price}$$

This formula can be transposed to yield units sold or average unit retail price:

$$\text{Units Sold} = \frac{\text{Sales Dollars}}{\text{Average Unit Retail Price}}$$

$$\text{Average Unit Retail Price} = \frac{\text{Sales Dollars}}{\text{Units Sold}}$$

In this exercise you will use the sell-through formula to calculate weekly sell-through percents for four weeks on three styles of skirts.

1. Open your *Application Exercises* file.

2. Insert a blank worksheet and type and format the values and labels as shown in Figure 6.4a.

3. Format cell ranges **D7:D9, F7:F9, H7:H9, J7:J9**, and **L7:L9** as **percent, decimal place 1**.

4. Format all other cells as **general, decimal place 0**.

5. Enter the formula in cell **D7** to calculate Week 1's sell through for Style 101 (Figure 6.4b).

6. Enter the formula in cell **F7** to calculate Week 2's sell through for Style 101 (Figure 6.4b).

    Note: For each week the units sold is included in the denominator as both a positive and a negative value which cancel each other. The formula can be simplified $=E7/(B7-C7)$ to yield the same result (Figure 6.4b).

7. Enter the formula in cell **H7** to calculate Week 3's sell through for Style 101 (Figure 6.4b).

    Note that the beginning inventory for Week 3 must be reduced by the number of units sold in Weeks 1 and 2 to arrive at the units on hand.

8. Enter the formula in cell **J7** to calculate Week 4's sell through for Style 101 (Figure 6.4b).

    Note that the beginning inventory for Week 4 must be reduced by the number of units sold in Weeks 1, 2, and 3 to arrive at the units on hand (Figure 6.4b).

9. Copy the formulas to **rows 8** and **9** (Figure 6.4c).

10. Now calculate sell through for the month. Enter the formula in cell **K7** to calculate the total units sold for the month (Figure 6.4c).

11. Enter the formula in cell **L7** to calculate sell through for the month (Figure 6.4c).

    Note that the month's sell-through is calculated simply by totaling each month's units sold (1178) and dividing by BOM units (3000) instead of $1178/(3000-260-268-300-350+1178)$. In this application the on-hands units at the end of the month are 1882. When the 1178 units sold are added to 1882, the total *beginning* on-hand units for the month is 3000.

12. Copy the formulas to rows **8** and **9** to calculate sell through for the other styles (Figure 6.4d).

13. Rename the sheet *Calculate Sell Through*.

14. Save your file.

Examine the sell-through percents for each style.

Note that the month's sell-through percents will not equal the sum of the weekly sell-through values. This is because each week's sell-through percent is calculated on a reduced inventory value. Recall that low sell-through percents result from too much inventory or too few sales. Observe the impacts of reduced inventory and increased sales on sell through.

15. The BOM for each style is 3,000 units, but the sell-through percents are different because of the variations in weekly sales. In cell **B8**, reduce the BOM units for Style 102 to 2,000 and note the increase in sell-through percents for *both* the weeks and month. Next, in cell **C8**, increase units sold to *175* and note a further increase in sell through.

16. Click *undo* twice to reverse the changes.

17. In cell **I8**, increase the units sold for Week 4 to 1,000 and observe a substantial increase in sell-through percents *only* for Week 4 and the month.

Note that the increase in Week 4 sales increased the overall sell through for the week and the month by reducing the amount of on-hand units available. Assuming that the season is not ending, this sell-through percent can direct buying or replenishment decisions for Style 102.

	A	B	C	D	E	F	G	H	I	J	K	L
1	*Calculate Sell-through Percent Using Unit Values*											
2	*Sell-through Percent = Units Sold / (Units On-Hand + Units Sold)*											
3												
4												
5				*Week 1*		*Week 2*		*Week 3*		*Week 4*		**Month**
6	Skirts	BOM Units	Units Sold	Sell-Through	Units Sold	Sell-Through	Units Sold	Sell-Through	Units Sold	Sell-Through	Total Units Sold	Sell-Through
7	*Style 101*	3000	260	?	268	?	300	?	350	?	?	?
8	*Style 102*	3000	75	?	80	?	95	?	100	?	?	?
9	*Style 103*	3000	200	?	198	?	200	?	275	?	?	?

Figure 6.4a Formula for sell-through percent

Figure 6.4b Formula for sell-through percent

	A	B	C	D	E	F	G	H	I	J	K	L
5			Week 1		Week 2		Week 3		Week 4		Month	
6	Skirts	BOM Units	Units Sold	Sell-Through	Units Sold	Sell-Through	Units Sold	Sell-Through	Units Sold	Sell-Through	Total Units Sold	Sell-Through
7	Style 101	3000	260	=C7/B7	268	=E7/(B7-C7)	300	=G7/(B7-C7-E7)	350	=I7/(B7-C7-E7-G7)	?	?
8	Style 102	3000	75	?	80	?	95	?	100	?	?	?
9	Style 103	3000	200	?	198	?	200	?	275	?	?	?

Figure 6.4c Formula for sell-through percent

	A	B	C	D	E	F	G	H	I	J	K	L
5			Week 1		Week 2		Week 3		Week 4		Month	
6	Skirts	BOM Units	Units Sold	Sell-Through	Units Sold	Sell-Through	Units Sold	Sell-Through	Units Sold	Sell-Through	Total Units Sold	Sell-Through
7	Style 101	3000	260	8.7%	268	9.8%	300	12.1%	350	16.1%	=SUM(C7,E7,G7,I7)	=K7/B7
8	Style 102	3000	75	2.5%	80	2.7%	95	3.3%	100	3.6%	?	?
9	Style 103	3000	200	6.7%	198	7.1%	200	7.7%	275	11.4%	?	?

Figure 6.4d Formula for sell-through percent

	A	B	C	D	E	F	G	H	I	J	K	L
5			Week 1		Week 2		Week 3		Week 4		Month	
6	Skirts	BOM Units	Units Sold	Sell-Through	Units Sold	Sell-Through	Units Sold	Sell-Through	Units Sold	Sell-Through	Total Units Sold	Sell-Through
7	Style 101	3000	260	8.7%	268	9.8%	300	12.1%	350	16.1%	1178	39.3%
8	Style 102	3000	75	2.5%	80	2.7%	95	3.3%	100	3.6%	350	11.7%
9	Style 103	3000	200	6.7%	198	7.1%	200	7.7%	275	11.4%	873	29.1%

Application Exercise 6.5 Use Formulas to Calculate a Sell-through Percent Using Unit-Sales Dollars

In this exercise you will use the sell-through formula to calculate sell-through percent using unit-sales *dollars*.

1. Open your *Application Exercises* file.

2. Insert a blank worksheet and type and format the values and labels as shown in Figure 6.5a.

3. Format cells **A10** and **B10** as **general**, **decimal place 0**.

4. Format cell **C10** as **currency**, **decimal place 0**.

5. Format cells **D10** and **E10** as **percent, decimal place 1**.

6. Insert the formula in cell **D10** to calculate sell through using unit *dollar* values (Figure 6.5b).

7. Insert the formula in cell **E10** to calculate sell through using *unit* values (Figure 6.5c).

8. Rename the sheet *Unit Dollars Sell Through*.

9. Save your file.

   Note that the sell-through percents are the same even though one formula uses unit *sales* and the other formula uses only units (Figure 6.5d).

10. In cell **C10**, change the average unit retail price to *$10.00* and notice that the sell-through percents are not impacted by the increase.

11. Click *undo* once to reverse the change.

12. In cell **A10**, change the units sold to *14,595* and note the increase in sell through.

13. Click *undo* once to reverse the change.

14. In cell **B10**, change the units on hand to *90,000* and note the decrease in sell-through percent.

Figure 6.5a

Formula for sell-through percent using unit sales

	A	B	C	D	E	F	G
1	*Calculate Sell-Through Percent Using Unit Dollar Values*						
2	*Sell-Through Percent = Sales Dollars / (Units On-Hand Dollars + Sales Dollars)*						
3	*Sales = Units * Average Unit Retail Price*						
4	*Average Unit Retail Price = Sales / Units*						
5	*Units = Sales / Average Unit Retail Price*						
6							
7							
8	Units Sold	Units On Hand	Average Unit Retail Price	Sell-Through *(use dollars)*	Sell-Through *(use units)*		
9							
10	4594	52549	$6.88	?	?		

Figure 6.5b

Formula for sell-through percent using unit sales

	A	B	C	D	E	F
8	Units Sold	Units On Hand	Average Unit Retail Price	Sell-Through *(use dollars)*	Sell-Through *(use units)*	
9						
10	4594	52549	$6.88	=A10*C10/(B10*C10+A10*C10)		

Figure 6.5c

Formula for sell-through percent using unit sales

	A	B	C	D	E	F
8	Units Sold	Units On Hand	Average Unit Retail Price	Sell-Through *(use dollars)*	Sell-Through *(use units)*	
9						
10	4594	52549	$6.88	8.0%	=A10/(B10+A10)	

Figure 6.5d

Formula for sell-through percent using unit sales

	A	B	C	D	E
8	Units Sold	Units On Hand	Average Unit Retail Price	Sell-Through *(use dollars)*	Sell-Through *(use units)*
9					
10	4594	52549	$6.88	8.0%	8.0%

SALES DISCOUNTS

Sales discounts are price adjustments that reflect a reduction in regular prices given to store employees as a fringe benefit. Sales discounts vary by retailer and product. Through sales discounts, employees are encouraged to purchase, use, and acquire knowledge about products. Sales discounts may also be given to customers at the sales manager's discretion. Sometimes a product has a flaw and the customer wants to buy it, but not at its full retail value. The sales manager may decide to deduct a percentage off the retail price. For example, if a 30-percent sales discount is offered on a retail price of $45, the resulting retail price of $31.50 would be calculated as follows:

$$\$45.00 * 30\% = \$13.50$$

$$\$45.00 - \$13.50 = \$31.50$$

Because sales discounts affect the value of the inventory, they must be planned if a desired profit is to be realized. Sales discounts are planned as a percent of planned sales. The percent planned is determined by store policy, industry average, or historical data. The total season's sales-discount dollars and the discount percent for each month are calculated with the following formulas:

Season's Sales Discount =
    Season's Planned Sales Discount Percent * Season's Planned Sales Dollars

$$\text{Month's Sales Discount Percent} = \frac{\text{Month's Discount Dollars}}{\text{Month's Sales Dollars}}$$

SHRINKAGE

Shortage or **shrinkage** are terms used to describe all instances in which items go missing from an inventory. The causes of shrinkage fall into four main categories: customer theft, employee theft, supplier underdelivery, and errors in recording and tracking inventory. Shrinkage affects the value of the inventory and must be planned. In planning, a shrinkage percent is estimated for the season and used to calculate monthly shrinkage dollars. Afterwards, a shrinkage percent of each month's sales is calculated. The formulas used are as follows:

Season's Shrinkage Dollars =
Season's Planned Shrinkage Percent * Season's Planned Sales Dollars

$$\text{Month's Shrinkage Percent of Sales} = \frac{\text{Month's Shrinkage Dollars}}{\text{Month's Sales Dollars}}$$

Despite the fact that a shrinkage percent is planned, the actual shortage that is realized at the end of an accounting period is determined by calculating the difference between the retail value of the book inventory and the physical inventory.

PLANNING REDUCTIONS

Reductions must be planned and controlled because they affect profit. In a dollar merchandise plan, sales and inventory are planned in dollars, and likewise, reductions are planned in retail dollar values and are calculated as a percentage of the planned sales. Reductions planning, whether for markdowns, sales discounts, or shrinkage, follows the same sequence and involves:

▶ calculating the season total

▶ planning percent distributions of the season total

▶ calculation of monthly dollar values

▶ calculation of month's percent of sales

Assignment Three

For your third assignment you will apply Excel skills and retail-math formulas to plan reductions based on sales that were planned in Assignment One. You will use functions, cell references, and absolute reference in your formulas.

1. Open your *Merchandise Budget* file.

2. Check your inventory plan and correct any formula errors.

3. Create a copy of your *Inventory Plan* sheet and rename the copy *Reductions Plan*. Position the *Reductions* sheet after the *Inventory* sheet.

Plan the season's reduction percents:

4. Insert a season markdown percent value of **17.3** percent in cell **C6**.

5. Insert a season sales discount percent value of **6.0** percent in cell **C7**.

6. Insert a season shrinkage percent value of **2.0** percent in cell **C8**.

Plan the season's markdown:

7. Apply a formula in cell **C25** to plan the season's total markdown dollars. Use cells **C6** and **C18** in your formula.

8. Enter a formula in cell **C27** to sum the markdown monthly distribution percents that you will plan in cells **D27:I27**.

9. Plan the following markdown distribution percents for each of the six months and type them in cells **D27:I27**:

FEB	MAR	APR	MAY	JUN	JUL
15.9%	16.2%	16.4%	16.7%	17.3%	17.5%

    Note that as you insert the percents, they are totaled in cell **C27**. If your total is less or more than 100 percent, check your values and formula.

10. Enter a formula with an absolute reference in cell **D25** to plan the dollar distribution of the season/total markdown value for FEB.

11. Copy the formula to other months in cells **E19:I19**.

12. Enter a formula in cell **C26** to calculate the season/total markdown percent of sales.

13. Copy the formula to the months in cells **D26:I26**.

Plan the sales discount:

14. In cell **C29**, apply a formula to plan the season's total employee-sales-discount dollars. Use cells **C7** and **C18** in your formula.

Enter a formula in cell **C31** to sum the monthly distribution percents that you will plan in cells **D31:I31**. Plan the following sales-discount distribution percents for each of the six months and type them in cells **D31:I31**. If your total is less or more than 100 percent, check your values and formulas.

FEB	MAR	APR	MAY	JUN	JUL
15.9%	16.1%	16.8%	17.3%	17.2%	16.7%

15. Enter a formula with an absolute reference in cell **D29** to plan the dollar distribution of the season/total sales-discount value for FEB.

16. Copy the formula to other months in cells **E29:I29**.

17. Enter a formula in cell **C30** to calculate the season/total sales discount percent of sales.

18. Copy the formula to the months in cells **D30:I30**.

Plan shrinkage:

19. In cell **C33**, apply a formula to calculate the season's total shrinkage dollars. Use cells **C8** and **C18** in your formula.

20. Enter a simple formula in cell **C35** to total the monthly shrinkage distribution percents that you will plan in cells **D35:I35**.

21. Plan the following shrinkage distribution percents for each of the six months and type them in cells **D35:I35**. If your total is less or more than 100 percent, check your values and formula.

FEB	MAR	APR	MAY	JUN	JUL
16.7%	16.7%	16.7%	16.6%	16.7%	16.6%

22. Enter a formula with an absolute reference in cell **D33** to calculate the dollar distribution of the season/total shrinkage value for FEB.

23. Copy the formula to the other months in cells **E33:I33**.

24. Enter a formula in cell **C34** to calculate the season/total shrinkage percent of sales.

25. Copy the formula to the months in cells **D34:I34**.

26. Save your file.

7 *Planning Purchases*

Chapter Objectives

After reading this chapter, you should be able to:

▶ Explain reasons for planning purchases.

▶ Distinguish between the retail value of purchases and the cost value of purchases.

▶ Define open-to-buy.

▶ Explain the importance of open-to-buy.

▶ Explain the difference between planned purchases and open-to-buy.

▶ Use Excel and structure retail formulas to calculate:
  · Planned retail purchases
  · Open-to-buy

KEY TERMS

On order is inventory paid for but not yet received by a retailer. Inventory on order is considered inventory available in calculation of open-to-buy.

Open-to-buy refers to the amount of inventory that can be purchased within a given time period without exceeding the planned inventory levels.

Overbought refers to having inventory available in excess of what is required for planned sales, reductions, and ending inventory.

Purchases refer to the dollars required to buy inventory for the planned sales, EOM, and reductions.

Purchases-at-cost refer to the dollar value of inventory when purchased by retailers to sell to customers.

Purchases-at-retail refer to the dollar value of inventory when sold to customers.

Planned **purchases** are the dollars required to purchase inventory and represent the fourth step in the development of a merchandise dollar plan. Purchases are sometimes referred to as *receipts* because the seller provides the retailer with a written acknowledgment of merchandise purchased. Purchases represent the amount of inventory that is planned for delivery to the store during a given period—usually monthly.

Purchases are planned in units and dollars. Unit purchase plans specify items to purchase and how the planned dollars should be spent relative to the number and assortment of items to meet needs for a designated time period. When purchases are planned in units, assortment factors such as size, brand, and color of the inventory are planned. This chapter discusses only dollar planning, which addresses the *amount of money* that should be planned for inventory purchases. When purchases are planned in dollars, they are planned at the retail value and at the cost value. **Purchases-at-retail** reflect the value of the inventory when sold to consumers. **Purchases-at-cost** reflect the retailer's cost in buying the inventory to sell.

THE PURPOSE OF PLANNING PURCHASES

The dollar merchandise budget provides plans for sales and inventory requirements. The purpose of planning purchases is to guide and control the investment in inventory. In the planning of purchases, control of investment is introduced through a formula that determines the amount of inventory based on what is needed and the amount that is already available:

Purchases = Merchandise Needed – Merchandise Available

The amount of inventory that is needed is based on the amount of sales, reductions, and EOM inventory that have been planned. Reductions, as discussed in Chapter Six, include markdowns, sales discounts, and shrinkage. The EOM is necessary, as it carries over as the following month's beginning inventory, covering that month's sales level. The merchandise available is the inventory available at the beginning of the month. The purchases formula can be expanded as follows:

Purchases = Sales + EOM + Reductions – BOM

This formula expresses the idea that if existing inventory is more than what is required to cover sales, reductions, and EOM, purchases should not be made until some of the existing inventory is sold or until sales, reductions, and EOM requirements are increased.

Application Exercise 7.1 Calculate Retail Purchases

You will use the purchases formula to calculate inventory requirements based on planned sales, inventory, and reductions values.

1. Open your *Application Exercises* file.
2. Insert a blank worksheet and type and format the values and labels as shown in Figure 7.1a.
3. Format cell **C14** as **currency, decimal place 0**, and enter the formula to calculate planned purchases (Figures 7.1b and 7.1c).
4. Rename the sheet *Purchases*.
5. Save your file.

Observe the impact on planned purchases when some of the planned values are increased and decreased:

6. Reduce sales to **$100,000**. Notice the decrease in required purchases.
7. Click *undo* to reverse the change.
8. Increase sales to **$222,000**, increase markdowns to **$20,000**, and increase sales discounts to **$7,000**. Notice the increase in required purchases.

9. Click *undo* three times to reverse the changes.

10. Increase the planned BOM to $275,000 and notice a negative value of ($46,560) for planned purchases, indicating that the buyer will be overbought and that purchases should not be made. This is because inventory available at the beginning of the month exceeds the $228,440 of inventory required to cover the month's planned sales, EOM, and reductions.

Figure 7.1a
Formula for calculating planned purchases

	A	B	C	D	E	F
1	*Calculate Planned Purchases*					
2	*Planned Purchases = Sales + EOM + Reductions - BOM*					
3						
4						
5	*Dollars Planned for Feb.*					
6						
7	Sales		$122,000			
8	EOM		$80,000			
9	Markdowns		$18,000			
10	Sales Discounts		$6,000			
11	Shrinkage		$2,440			
12	BOM		$75,000			
13						
14	**Planned Purchases**		?			

Figure 7.1b
Formula for calculating planned purchases

	A	B	C	D
5	*Dollars Planned for Feb.*			
6				
7	Sales		$122,000	
8	EOM		$80,000	
9	Markdowns		$18,000	
10	Sales Discounts		$6,000	
11	Shrinkage		$2,440	
12	BOM		$75,000	
13				
14	**Planned Purchases**		=C7+C8+C9+C10+C11-C12	

Figure 7.1c

Formula for
calculating planned
purchases

	A	B	C	D
5	*Dollars Planned for Feb.*			
6				
7	Sales		$122,000	
8	EOM		$80,000	
9	Markdowns		$18,000	
10	Sales Discounts		$6,000	
11	Shrinkage		$2,440	
12	BOM		$75,000	
13				
14	**Planned Purchases**		**$153,440**	

OPEN-TO-BUY (OTB)

Open-to-buy is the amount of inventory that can be purchased within a given time period without exceeding the planned inventory levels. Open-to-buy is related to purchases because it controls inventory investment for a specific period. OTB differs from purchases in that it serves as a tool to both *control* and *balance* inventory. To balance inventory, OTB calculates the dollar amount of *additional* inventory that can be purchased without exceeding the purchases that were originally planned.

Open-to-buy is indicative that inventory is turning and meeting planned sales goals. OTB is important because it allows retail buyers to make additional purchases during the month that can be used to reorder popular items; to purchases new, fast-selling *hot items*; and to take advantage of special offers from vendors.

Inventory requirements are planned for an entire month, but actual purchases are made and scheduled for delivery at intervals throughout the month. Therefore, OTB calculation is done *after* the month begins and at intervals during the month. Open-to-buy calculated at the beginning of the month requires determining the planned purchases for the month and subtracting outstanding purchases for the month:

OTB = (Sales + EOM + Reductions – BOM) – Month's Inventory on Order

Inventory that is **on order** and scheduled to be received during the month must be considered because even though purchases are not physically in the stockroom, there is a financial obligation for payment. A negative OTB indicates that the retailer is **overbought** and additional purchases should not be made because enough inventory is available to cover planned requirements for the month.

Application Exercise 7.2 Calculate Open-to-Buy at the Beginning of the Month

You will use the OTB formula to calculate additional purchases that can be made at the beginning of the month given the sales, EOM, reductions, and BOM that have been planned and the inventory that is on order for the month.

1.   Open your *Application Exercises* file.

2.   Make a copy of your *Purchases* sheet.

3.   *Delete* the formula in cell **C14** (Figure 7.2a).

4.   In cell **A13**, type the label *Feb. on-order* (Figure 7.2a).

5.   In cell **A14**, type the label *Feb. OTB* (Figure 7.2a).

6.   Format cell **C13** as **currency, decimal place 0**, and type in an on-order value of *$50,000* (Figure 7.2b).

7.   Format cell **C14** as **currency, decimal place 0**, and enter the formula to calculate open-to-buy (Figures 7.2c and 7.2d).

8.   Rename the sheet *OTB at Beginning of Month*.

9.   Save your file.

Observe the impact on OTB when the on-order value is increased and decreased:

10.   In cell **C13**, change *Feb. on-order* to **$100,000** and note the substantial decrease in OTB for the month.

11.   Click *undo* to reverse the change.

12.   Change *Feb. on-order* to **$25,000** and note the increase in OTB.

13.   Click *undo* to reverse the change.

14.   Change *Feb. on-order* to *$0.00* and note the OTB is $153,440, the same as the planned purchases calculated in Application Exercise 7.1.

Observe ways of increasing OTB at the beginning of the month:

15.   In cell **C8**, change the EOM to *$90,000* and note the increase in OTB for FEB.

Note that OTB is increased because FEB's planned-purchases value is increased to $163,440. The additional $10,000 in EOM will be carried into the next month (MAR) as beginning inventory, allowing an extra $10,000 to be used for additional purchases for FEB.

16. Click *undo* to reverse the change.

Note that increases in merchandise needed, e.g., planned sales, EOM, or reductions, will increase the OTB for the beginning of the month.

	A	B	C	D	E	F	G	H
1	*Calculate OTB for Beginning of Month*							
2	*OTB = (Sales + EOM + Reductions - BOM) - Month's Inventory on-Order*							
3								
4								
5	*Dollars Planned for Feb.*							
6								
7	Sales		$122,000					
8	EOM		$80,000					
9	Markdowns		$18,000					
10	Sales discounts		$6,000					
11	Shrinkage		$2,440					
12	BOM		$75,000					
13	*Feb. on-Order*							
14	**Feb. OTB**		?					

Figure 7.2a Formula for calculating open-to-buy at the beginning of the month

Figure 7.2b
Formula for calculating open-to-buy at the beginning of the month

	A	B	C	D	E
5	*Dollars Planned for Feb.*				
6					
7	Sales		$122,000		
8	EOM		$80,000		
9	Markdowns		$18,000		
10	Sales discounts		$6,000		
11	Shrinkage		$2,440		
12	BOM		$75,000		
13	*Feb. on-Order*		$50,000		
14	**Feb. OTB**		?		

Figure 7.2c

Formula for
calculating open-to-
buy at the beginning
of the month

	A	B	C	D	E
5	*Dollars Planned for Feb.*				
6					
7	Sales		$122,000		
8	EOM		$80,000		
9	Markdowns		$18,000		
10	Sales discounts		$6,000		
11	Shrinkage		$2,440		
12	BOM		$75,000		
13	*Feb. on-Order*		$50,000		
14	**Feb. OTB**		=(C7+C8+C9+C10+C11–C12)–C13		

Figure 7.2d

Formula for
calculating open-to-
buy at the beginning
of the month

	A	B	C	D	E
5	*Dollars Planned for Feb.*				
6					
7	Sales		$122,000		
8	EOM		$80,000		
9	Markdowns		$18,000		
10	Sales discounts		$6,000		
11	Shrinkage		$2,440		
12	BOM		$75,000		
13	*Feb. on-Order*		$50,000		
14	**Feb. OTB**		**$103,440**		

When open-to-buy is calculated during the month, the calculation can be
based on the purchases that have been planned for the month or the planned
EOM inventory as illustrated in the following formulas:

OTB for the Balance of a Month Based on Purchases =
> Planned Purchases – (Inventory Received to Date
> + Month's Inventory on Order)

OTB for the Balance of a Month Based on EOM =
> Planned EOM + Planned Sales + Planned Reductions
> – (Inventory on Hand + Month's Inventory on Order)

Application Exercise 7.3 Calculate OTB for the Balance of a Month Based on Planned Purchases

In this exercise you will calculate OTB for the balance of a month using the planned purchases and receipt of some of the month's previously ordered inventory.

1. Open your *Application Exercises* file.

2. Insert a blank worksheet and type and format the values and labels as shown in Figure 7.3a.

3. Format cell **B13** as **currency**, **decimal place**, **0**.

4. Enter the formula in cell **B13** to calculate open-to-buy for the balance of the month (Figures 7.3b and 7.3c).

	A	B	C	D	E	F	G	H
1	Calculate OTB for Balance of Month Based on Planned Purchases							
2	OTB Balance = Planned Purchases - (Inventory Received to Date + Month's Inventory On-Order)							
3								
4								
5	Calculate OTB as of March 14							
6								
7	Planned Sales *(March 1-31)*	$165,000		March Inventory On-Order	$80,000			
8	Planned Markdown *(March 1-31)*	$26,000		Receipts *(March 1-14)*	$30,000			
9	Planned Sales Discounts *(March 1-31)*	$8,750						
10	Planned EOM *(March)*	$75,000						
11	BOM *(March 1)*	$140,000						
12								
13	OTB *as of 3/14*	?						

Figure 7.3a Formula for calculating open-to-buy based on planned purchases

	A	B	C	D	E
5	Calculate OTB as of March 14				
6					
7	Planned Sales *(March 1-31)*	$165,000		March Inventory On-Order	$80,000
8	Planned Markdown *(March 1-31)*	$26,000		Receipts *(March 1-14)*	$30,000
9	Planned Sales Discounts *(March 1-31)*	$8,750			
10	Planned EOM *(March)*	$75,000			
11	BOM *(March 1)*	$140,000			
12					
13	OTB *as of 3/14*	=(B7+B8+B9+B10-B11)-(E8+E7)			

Figure 7.3b Formula for calculating open-to-buy based on planned purchases

	A	B	C	D	E
5	*Calculate OTB as of March 14*				
6					
7	Planned Sales *(March 1-31)*	$165,000		March Inventory On-Order	$80,000
8	Planned Markdown *(March 1-31)*	$26,000		Receipts *(March 1-14)*	$30,000
9	Planned Sales Discounts *(March 1-31)*	$8,750			
10	Planned EOM *(March)*	$75,000			
11	BOM *(March 1)*	$140,000			
12					
13	**OTB** *as of 3/14*	**$24,750**			

Figure 7.3c Formula for calculating open-to-buy based on planned purchases

5. Rename the sheet *OTB Balance_Purchases*.

6. Save your file.

   Note that the planned purchase value is not provided, so it is calculated in the first part of the formula and then the inventory on hand and inventory on order are subtracted to yield OTB for the balance of the month.

Application Exercise 7.4 Calculate OTB for the Balance of a Month Based on Planned EOM

In this exercise you will calculate OTB for the balance of a month. The calculation will be based on the month's planned EOM and the remainder of the month's planned sales and reductions.

1. Open your *Application Exercises* file.

2. Insert a blank worksheet and type and format the values and labels as shown in Figure 7.4a.

3. Format cell **B14** as **currency, decimal place 0**.

4. Enter the formula in cell **B14** to calculate open-to-buy for the balance of the month (Figures 7.4b and 7.4c).

5. Rename the sheet *OTB Balance EOM*.

6. Save your file.

As illustrated in Application Exercise 7.2, an increase in either the planned EOM, sales, or reductions will increase OTB.

	A	B	C	D	E	F	G	H
1	*Calculate OTB for Balance of Month Based on Planned EOM*							
2	*OTB Balance = (Planned EOM + Planned Sales Balance + Planned Reductions Balance)*							
3	*- (Inventory on-Hand + Month's Inventory on-Order)*							
4								
5	*Calculate OTB as of April 11*							
6								
7	Planned Sales (April 1-30)	$92,000		Planned EOM (April)	$85,000			
8	Actual Sales *as of 4/11*	$53,281		Inventory On-Hand *4/11*	$20,000			
9	Planned Markdown (April 1-30)	$12,953		April Inventory On-Order	$60,000			
10	Actual Markdown *as of 4/11*	$5,000						
11	Planned Sales Discounts (April 1-30)	$9,000						
12	Actual Sales Discounts *as of 4/11*	$3,000						
13								
14	**OTB** *as of 4/11*	?						

Figure 7.4a Formula for calculating open-to-buy based on planned EOM

	A	B	C	D	E
5	*Calculate OTB as of April 11*				
6					
7	Planned Sales (April 1-30)	$92,000		Planned EOM (April)	$85,000
8	Actual Sales *as of 4/11*	$53,281		Inventory On-Hand *4/11*	$20,000
9	Planned Markdown (April 1-30)	$12,953		April Inventory On-Order	$60,000
10	Actual Markdown *as of 4/11*	$5,000			
11	Planned Sales Discounts (April 1-30)	$9,000			
12	Actual Sales Discounts *as of 4/11*	$3,000			
13					
14	**OTB** *as of 4/11*	=E7+(B7-B8)+(B9-B10)+(B11-B12)-(E8+E9)			

Figure 7.4b Formula for calculating open-to-buy based on planned EOM

	A	B	C	D	E
5	*Calculate OTB as of April 11*				
6					
7	Planned Sales (April 1-30)	$92,000		Planned EOM (April)	$85,000
8	Actual Sales *as of 4/11*	$53,281		Inventory On-Hand *4/11*	$20,000
9	Planned Markdown (April 1-30)	$12,953		April Inventory On-Order	$60,000
10	Actual Markdown *as of 4/11*	$5,000			
11	Planned Sales Discounts (April 1-30)	$9,000			
12	Actual Sales Discounts *as of 4/11*	$3,000			
13					
14	**OTB** *as of 4/11*	$57,672			

Figure 7.4c Formula for calculating open-to-buy based on planned EOM

Assignment Four

For your fourth assignment, you will apply Excel skills and retail-math formulas to plan retail purchases.

1. Open your *Merchandise Budget* file. Check your reductions plan and correct any formula errors.

2. Create a copy of your *Reductions Plan* sheet and rename the copy *Retail Purchases Plan*. Position the *Purchases* sheet after the *Reductions* sheet.

3. In cell **D37**, enter a formula to calculate planned purchases for FEB.

4. Copy the formula to the other months in **E37:I37**.

5. In cell **C37**, enter a formula to sum the monthly planned purchases.

6. Save your file.

8 *Planning Markups*

Chapter Objectives

After reading this chapter, you should be able to:

▶ Explain the importance of markup.

▶ Differentiate between the types of markup.

▶ Explain how markup is calculated and expressed.

▶ Provide an example to illustrate the role of markup in the calculation of price.

▶ Use Excel and structure retail formulas to calculate:

- Markup dollars
- Markup percents
- Markups on inventory consisting of various units, retail prices, and cost prices
- Cost price using complement of markup
- Retail price using complement of markup
- Initial markup

- Cumulative markup
- Maintained markup using planned reductions and initial markup percents

▶ Allowable reduction percents using maintained markups and initial markup.

KEY TERMS

Billed cost is the cost of merchandise that is reflected on the vendor's invoice.

Cost price refers to the amount paid by retailers in purchasing merchandise for sale.

Cost complement or **cost percent** is the difference between the retail value of 100 percent and the markup percent. The cost percent is used to convert retail price to cost, or cost price to retail.

Cumulative markup (CUMU) is the average markup achieved over a specific time period on existing and new inventory. A cumulative markup is the difference between the total cost and the total retail values.

Earned cash discounts are the reductions in the cost of inventory given by the vendor to the retailer for meeting specific conditions of purchase. The discount is expressed as a percent of the billed cost.

Ending inventory refers to the value of inventory remaining at the end of an accounting period.

Freight refers to the cost associated with getting merchandise shipped to a retailer's place of business. For retailers, a freight charge is calculated as a percent of merchandise cost.

Gross Cost is the billed cost of merchandise adjusted by trade discounts. Gross cost includes freight cost.

Initial markup (IMU) is the first markup applied to inventory cost to establish the original retail price.

Maintained markup (MMU) is the markup achieved at the time of sale. A maintained markup is the difference between the actual selling price and the cost.

Markup is the amount added to the cost of an item to determine its retail price.

Markup cancellations are price adjustments that cancel all or part of an addition to a previous markup. A markup cancellation does not lower a price below its original retail price.

Net transfer refers to the difference between transfers in and transfers out. *Transfers* refer to inventory that is moved in and out of departments within retail organizations.

Opening inventory refers to the cost and retail values of inventory available at the beginning of an accounting period.

Purchases are merchandise bought by retailers for resale to customers.

Retail price refers to the price at which merchandise is sold.

Retail method of inventory valuation is a perpetual book-inventory valuation method that uses the retail value of an ending inventory and cumulative markup to estimate the inventory's ending cost value.

Returns are merchandise returned to vendors for credit or refunds. Returns reduce the value of inventory handled.

Upward revisions of markup are increases in the markup to establish a higher retail price for competitive reasons, to make up for increases in cost, or to improve perceptions of product quality.

Markup is an amount added to an item's cost to determine its retail price. The concept of *markup* is illustrated in the following formulas:

Cost + Markup = Retail

Retail – Markup = Cost

Retail – Cost = Markup

HOW MARKUP IS CALCULATED AND EXPRESSED

Markup is calculated in dollars. Most often, markup is expressed as a percentage of the retail value of a product, although some retailers express markup as a percentage of the cost value. Formulas for dollar markup and percent are:

Dollar Markup = Retail Price – Cost Price

$$\text{Markup Percent on Retail Price} = \frac{\text{Dollar Markup}}{\text{Retail Price}}$$

$$\text{Markup Percent on Cost Price} = \frac{\text{Dollar Markup}}{\text{Cost Price}}$$

Application Exercise 8.1 Calculate a Markup Percentage on a Retail Price and on a Cost Price

You will use the markup formulas to calculate markup percentage on retail and on cost values.

1. Open your *Application Exercises* file.

2. Insert a blank worksheet and type and format the values and labels as shown in Figure 8.1a.

3. Format cell range **D7:D9** as **currency, decimal place 0**.

4. Format cell range **E7:E9** as **percent, decimal place = 1**.

5. Enter the formula in cell **D7** to calculate dollar markup (Figure 8.1b).

6. Copy the formula to cell **D9** (Figure 8.1b).

7. Enter the formula in cell **E7** to calculate markup percent on retail (Figures 8.1b and 8.1c).

8. Enter the formula in cell **E9** to calculate markup percent on cost (Figures 8.1b and 8.1c).

9. Rename the sheet *Markup on Retail & Cost*.

10. Save your file.

11. Change the retail price in cells **B7** and **B9** to $70.

    Note that the dollar markup will always be the same for markup on retail and markup on cost. The markup percent calculated on cost is always higher because the cost price is always lower than the retail price.

Figure 8.1a
Formula for calculating a markup percentage on retail prices and costs

	A	B	C	D	E	F
1	*Calculate Markup Percentage on Retail Price and on Cost Price*					
2	*Dollar Markup = Retail Price - Cost Price*					
3	*Markup Percentage on Retail = Dollar Markup / Retail Price*					
4	*Markup Percentage on Cost = Dollar Markup / Cost Price*					
5						
6		Retail Price	Cost Price	Dollar Markup	Markup Percent	
7	*Percentage on Retail*	$60	$35	?	?	
8						
9	*Percentage on Cost*	$60	$35	?	?	

Figure 8.1b
Formula for
calculating a markup
percentage on retail
prices and costs

	A	B	C	D	E
6		Retail Price	Cost Price	Dollar Markup	Markup Percent
7	*Percentage on Retail*	$60	$35	=B7-C7	=D7/B7
8					
9	*Percentage on Cost*	$60	$35	=B9-C9	=D9/C9

Figure 8.1c
Formula for
calculating a markup
percentage on retail
prices and costs

	A	B	C	D	E
6		Retail Price	Cost Price	Dollar Markup	Markup Percent
7	*Percentage on Retail*	$60	$35	$25	41.7%
8					
9	*Percentage on Cost*	$60	$35	$25	71.4%

The formulas above can be used to calculate markup percent on one item or an entire inventory if the **cost price** and **retail price** do not change. However, on an inventory consisting of a variety of items, units, and prices, markup percent must be calculated on the total-dollar markup. Total-dollar markup is calculated as follows:

Total Retail Price = Retail Price * Units

Total Cost Price = Cost Price * Units

Total-Dollar Markup = Total Retail Price – Total Cost Price

As illustrated in the above formulas, calculating total-dollar markup requires that the number of units be used to calculate the total retail and total cost values.

Application Exercise 8.2 Calculate a Total Markup Percent on Inventory

In this exercise you will use the markup formulas to calculate a total markup on inventory consisting of various units, retail prices, and cost prices.

1. Open your *Application Exercises* file.

2. Insert a blank worksheet and type and format the values and labels as shown in Figure 8.2a.

3. Format cell ranges **E9:G12** and **E16:F18** as **currency, decimal place 0**.

4. Format cell ranges **H9:H12** and **F16:F18** as **percent, decimal place 1**.

5. Enter the formula in cell **E9** to calculate the total retail price for jackets (Figure 8.2b).

6. Enter the formula in cell **F9** to calculate the total cost price for jackets (Figure 8.2b).

7. Enter the formula in cell **G9** to calculate the total dollar markup for jackets (Figure 8.2b).

8. Enter the formula in cell **H9** to calculate the markup percent on retail for jackets (Figure 8.2b).

9. Copy the formulas to rows **10** and **11** (Figure 8.2c).

10. Enter the formula in cell **E12** to sum the retail prices. Copy the formula to cells **F12** and **G12** (Figure 8.2c).

11. Enter the formula in cell **H12** to calculate the total markup percent on retail (Figure 8.2c).

12. In cell **E16**, enter the formula to calculate a single-dollar markup for jackets. In cell **F16**, enter the formula to calculate the markup percent on retail for jackets. Copy the formulas to rows **17** and **18** (Figures 8.2c and 8.2d).

	A	B	C	D	E	F	G	H
1	*Calculate Markup Percent on Inventory with Varying Units and Prices*							
2	*Total Retail Price = Retail price * Units*							
3	*Total Cost Price = Cost Price * Units*							
4	*Total Dollar Markup = Total Retail Price - Total Cost Price*							
5	*Total Markup Percentage on Retail = Total Dollar Markup / Total Retail Price*							
6								
7	*Inventory with Different Units, Retail and Cost Prices*							
8		# Units	Retail Price	Cost Price	*Total Retail Price*	*Total Cost Price*	*Total Dollar Markup*	Markup Percent
9	Jackets	10	$128	$52	?	?	?	?
10	Skirts	25	$89	$35	?	?	?	?
11	Blouses	18	$48	$22	?	?	?	?
12	*Total*				?	?	?	?
13								
14	*One Unit with One Retail and One Cost Price*							
15		# Units	Retail Price	Cost Price	Dollar Markup	Markup Percent		
16	Jackets	1	$128	$52	?	?		
17	Skirts	1	$89	$35	?	?		
18	Blouses	1	$48	$22	?	?		

Figure 8.2a Formula for calculating a markup on inventory with varying units and prices

	A	B	C	D	E	F	G	H
7	Inventory with Different Units, Retail and Cost Prices							
8		# Units	Retail Price	Cost Price	Total Retail Price	Total Cost Price	Total Dollar Markup	Markup Percent
9	Jackets	10	$128	$52	=C9*B9	=D9*B9	=E9-F9	=G9/E9
10	Skirts	25	$89	$35	?	?	?	?
11	Blouses	18	$48	$22	?	?	?	?
12	Total				?	?	?	?
13								
14	One Unit with One Retail and One Cost Price							
15		# Units	Retail Price	Cost Price	Dollar Markup	Markup Percent		
16	Jackets	1	$128	$52	?	?		
17	Skirts	1	$89	$35	?	?		
18	Blouses	1	$48	$22	?	?		

Figure 8.2b Formula for calculating a markup on inventory with varying units and prices

	A	B	C	D	E	F	G	H
7	Inventory with Different Units, Retail and Cost Prices							
8		# Units	Retail Price	Cost Price	Total Retail Price	Total Cost Price	Total Dollar Markup	Markup Percent
9	Jackets	10	$128	$52	$1,280	$520	$760	59.38%
10	Skirts	25	$89	$35	$2,225	$875	$1,350	60.67%
11	Blouses	18	$48	$22	$864	$396	$468	54.17%
12	Total				=SUM(E9:E11)	=SUM(F9:F11)	=SUM(G9:G11)	=G12/E12
13								
14	One Unit with One Retail and One Cost Price							
15		# Units	Retail Price	Cost Price	Dollar Markup	Markup Percent		
16	Jackets	1	$128	$52	=C16-D16	=E16/C16		
17	Skirts	1	$89	$35	=C17-D17	=E17/C17		
18	Blouses	1	$48	$22	=C18-D18	=E18/C18		

Figure 8.2c Formula for calculating a markup on inventory with varying units and prices

13. Rename the sheet *Markup on Inventory*.

14. Save your file.

Note that the total markup in cell H12 is not a sum or average of the individual markups on jackets, skirts, and blouses. It is calculated as the *total-dollar* markup.

	A	B	C	D	E	F	G	H
7	*Inventory with Different Units, Retail and Cost Prices*							
8		# Units	Retail Price	Cost Price	*Total Retail Price*	*Total Cost Price*	*Total Dollar Markup*	Markup Percent
9	Jackets	10	$128	$52	$1,280	$520	$760	59.38%
10	Skirts	25	$89	$35	$2,225	$875	$1,350	60.67%
11	Blouses	18	$48	$22	$864	$396	$468	54.17%
12	*Total*				**$4,369**	**$1,791**	**$2,578**	59.01%
13								
14	*One Unit with One Retail and One Cost Price*							
15		# Units	Retail Price	Cost Price	Dollar Markup	Markup Percent		
16	Jackets	1	$128	$52	$76	**59.38%**		
17	Skirts	1	$89	$35	$54	**60.67%**		
18	Blouses	1	$48	$22	$26	**54.17%**		

Figure 8.2d Formula for calculating a markup on inventory with varying units and prices

Compare the markup values in cells **F16:F18** with those in cells **H9:H11**.

Note that when the number of units varies but individual cost and individual retail values do not change, the markup percent is the same whether it is calculated for one unit or multiple units (Figure 8.2d).

USING MARKUP PERCENT TO CALCULATE PRICES

A retail price is composed of a markup component and a cost component. A markup percent, when added to a **cost percent**, equals the retail price, which is always 100 percent. The cost percent is referred to as the **cost complement** of the markup. It is calculated by subtracting the markup percent from the retail percent as shown in the following example:

Retail	100.00%
– Markup	40.00%
= Cost	60.00%

When inventory purchases are planned at the retail value, a retailer must be able to determine the maximum amount to pay for merchandise in order to achieve a desired markup. Sometimes buyers have opportunities to purchase inventory at a specific cost and need to determine the retail price that will result from a required markup. If merchandise is purchased at a specific cost and has a predetermined markup, the retail price is determined by dividing the cost price by the complement of the markup as follows:

$$Retail = \frac{Cost}{(100\% - Markup\%)}$$

When there is a predetermined retail price, the cost price is calculated by multiplying the retail price by the complement of the markup as follows:

$$Cost = Retail * (100\% - Markup\%)$$

Application Exercise 8.3 **Use a Markup Percent to Calculate Cost and Retail Prices**

In this exercise you will use a markup percent to calculate unit costs and retail prices.

1.   Open your *Application Exercises* file.

2.   Insert a blank worksheet and type and format the values and labels as shown in Figure 8.3a.

3.   Format cells **D6:D7** and **B12:B14** as **currency, decimal place 0**.

4.   In cell **D6**, enter the formula to calculate the retail price of *one pair* of gloves. Copy the formula to cell **D7** (Figures 8.3b and 8.3c).

Figure 8.3a
Formula for
calculating retail
prices and costs
using a desired
markup percent

	A	B	C	D
1	*Calculate Price with a Markup Percent*			
2	*Retail Price = Cost / (100 - Markup Percent)*			
3	*Cost Price = Retail * (100 - Markup Percent)*			
4	*Calculate Retail Price*			
5		Cost *(per Dozen)*	Markup	**Retail Price** *(per Pair)*
6	Gloves	$50	65.0%	?
7	Socks	$35	50.0%	?
8				
9				
10	*Calculate Cost Price*			
11		**Cost Price** *(each)*	Markup	Retail
12	Pants	?	65.0%	$189
13	Shirts	?	50.0%	$83
14	Jackets	?	68.0%	$120

Figure 8.3b

Formula for
calculating retail
prices and costs
using a desired
markup percent

	A	B	C	D
4	*Calculate Retail Price*			
5		Cost *(per Dozen)*	Markup	**Retail Price** *(per Pair)*
6	Gloves	$50	65.0%	=(B6/12)/(1-C6)
7	Socks	$35	50.0%	?
8				
9				
10	*Calculate Cost Price*			
11		**Cost Price** *(each)*	Markup	Retail
12	Pants	=D12*(1-C12)	65.0%	$189
13	Shirts	?	50.0%	$83
14	Jackets	?	68.0%	$120

Figure 8.3c

Formula for
calculating retail
prices and costs
using a desired
markup percent

	A	B	C	D
4	*Calculate Retail Price*			
5		Cost *(per Dozen)*	Markup	**Retail Price** *(per Pair)*
6	Gloves	$50	65.0%	**$11.90**
7	Socks	$35	50.0%	**$5.83**
8				
9				
10	*Calculate Cost Price*			
11		**Cost Price** *(each)*	Markup	Retail
12	Pants	**$66.15**	65.0%	$189
13	Shirts	**$41.50**	50.0%	$83
14	Jackets	**$38.40**	68.0%	$120

Note that gloves and socks are priced by the dozen and the formula is structured to calculate unit cost first and then convert the cost price to the retail price.

5. In cell **B12**, enter the formula to calculate the cost price for pants. Copy the formula to cells **B13:B14** (Figures 8.3b and 8.3c).

6. Rename the sheet *Calculate Prices with Markup*.

7. Save your file.

TYPES OF MARKUP

Planning markups is important because a markup must be large enough to result in a retail price that covers expenses and profit as illustrated in this basic profit formula:

Retail Price
– Cost Price
= Markup
– Expenses
= Profit

There are three types of markups that retailers consider when planning. They are:

► Initial markup

► Maintained markup

► Cumulative markup

Initial Markup (IMU)

As previously indicated, a markup is the difference between the cost and retail price. **Initial Markup** is the first markup applied to merchandise cost and establishes the original retail price. Initial markup is planned *prior* to selling and is based on *planned net sales*. It is this markup that retailers hope to achieve on the sale of inventory. Once a retail price is established, the markup is sometimes adjusted upward. **Upward revisions of markup** may be required to establish a higher retail price for competitive reasons, to make up for increases in inventory cost, or to improve customers' perceptions of product quality. After a price is increased by an addition to its markup, all or part of the addition may later be reduced through a **markup cancellation**. A markup cancellation is a price adjustment, but, unlike a markdown, it does not lower the price below the original retail price.

Maintained Markup (MMU)

Maintained Markup is the markup that is achieved on *actual sales* as determined by the prices at which products are sold. A maintained markup is defined as the difference between the actual sales and the cost of merchandise. A relationship exists between a maintained markup and an initial markup in that a maintained markup is that part of the IMU that remains over time. During a season, not all products sell at the original retail price. For a variety of reasons, a sales value planned from an original retail price is eroded by markdowns, sales discounts, and/or shrinkage. Though the cost price does not change, retail-price erosion produces a lower sales value, which results in a lower or *maintained* markup.

A lower markup impacts profit. As illustrated in the following example, a profit of $5 may result from planned sales of $45 and a cost price of $20:

Planned Retail Sales Price	$45
Cost Price	– $20
Initial Markup	$25
Expenses	– $20
Profit	$5

In the following calculation, planned sales are reduced to *actual sales* of $40 as a result of reductions, and produce a profit of $2:

Planned Retail Sales Price	$45
Markdown	– $3
Sales Discounts	– $1
Shrinkage	– $1
Actual Retail Sales	$40
Cost Price	– $20
Maintained Markup	$22
Expenses	– $20
Profit	$2

A maintained markup can be viewed as the difference between the initial markup and reductions because it is markdowns, sales discounts, and shortages that decrease the retail price. As shown in the following example, if there are no reductions from the retail price, the initial markup and the maintained markup will be the same:

Initial Markup	65%
Markdown	(0%)
Sales Discounts	(0%)
Shrinkage	(0%)
Maintained Markup	65%

Planning Initial Markup Percent

As illustrated by the two calculations of profit, a maintained markup is based on actual sales and is a key determinant of profitability because it must be large enough to cover expenses and profit. Therefore, when planning the initial markup, it is critical that the resulting retail price include reductions to retail as well as the maintained markup. The initial markup is calculated as a percent as illustrated in the following formulas:

$$\text{Initial Markup} = \frac{\text{Maintained Markup} + \text{Reductions}}{\text{Net Sales} + \text{Reductions}}$$

or

$$\text{Initial Markup} = \frac{\text{(Expenses + Profit + Markdown + Sales Discount + Shrinkage)}}{\text{(Net Sales + Markdown + Sales Discount + Shrinkage)}}$$

In addition to reductions, alterations or workroom expenses are sometimes required to prepare products for sale and must be included in the initial markup. For example, some retailers offer customer services to alter or assemble merchandise and will cover all or part of the costs associated with labor, materials, and supplies. Alterations result in an added expense and, when included in the calculation of IMU, will increase the required markup percent.

Earned cash discounts are deductions from the **billed cost** of inventory given by vendors to retailers to encourage prompt payment of invoices within a given time period. Cash discounts reduce inventory cost and some retailers factor them into their calculation of the initial markup. When cash discounts are included in the calculation of an initial markup, they result in a lower markup requirement than when they are omitted. Cash discounts are not guaranteed, so if the condition of prompt payment is not met, the discount is lost. It is for this reason that some retailers elect to not include cash discounts when calculating IMU, considering them to be additional income and using this type of discount as a profit cushion. When alteration and workroom expenses are present, the initial markup formula is:

$$\text{Initial Markup} = \frac{\text{Expenses + Profit + Reductions + Alterations – Cash Discounts}}{\text{Net Sales + Reductions}}$$

How the Initial Markup Is Used in Planning

The initial markup percent is used to determine the *maximum cost* price or the *minimum retail* price required on new purchases to accomplish a profit objective. A retail price is composed of a markup and a cost. As illustrated in the following example, when the markup percent is subtracted from the retail percent of 100, the result is the cost percent:

	%
Retail	100.00%
Markup (IMU)	– 53.94%
Cost	46.06%

The cost percent—the complement of the IMU—is used to calculate the cost or retail price as shown in the following formulas:

$$\text{Cost} = \text{Retail} * (100\ \% - \text{IMU}\ \%)$$

$$\text{Retail} = \frac{\text{Cost}}{(100\ \% - \text{IMU}\ \%)}$$

In this exercise you will use the formulas to calculate IMU percent, retail price, and cost price.

1. Open your *Application Exercises* file.

2. Insert a blank worksheet and type and format the values and labels as shown in Figure 8.4a.

3. Format cells **C14** and **C15** as **percent, decimal place 1**.

4. Format cells **G9** and **G11** as **currency, decimal places 2**.

5. Insert the formula in cell **C14** to calculate the IMU *with* a cash discount (Figure 8.4b).

6. Insert the formula in cell **C15** to calculate the IMU *without* a cash discount (Figure 8.4b).

7. Rename the sheet *Calculate IMU*.

8. Save your file.

    Note that the IMU that is calculated without cash discounts is higher than the IMU calculated with cash discounts (Figure 8.4c).

9. Enter the formula in cell **G9** to calculate the *cost price*. Use the IMU percent in cell **C15** (Figure 8.4c).

10. Enter the formula in cell **G11** to calculate the *retail price*. Use the IMU percent in cell **C15** (Figure 8.4c).

11. Save your file.

    Note that a percent value for sales is not provided in Figure 8.4a, but is accounted for in the formulas as 100 percent (Figure 8.4b). Observe the impact of an increase in profit, expenses, and reductions on IMU, cost price, and retail price.

12. Increase the profit percent in cell **B8** to *8 percent* and note that the IMU is increased, the cost price is decreased, and the retail price is increased.

13. Click *undo* to reverse the change.

14. Change the alteration percent in cell **D9** to *0 percent* and note that the IMU is decreased, the cost price is increased, and the retail price is decreased.

15. Click *undo* to reverse the change.

Observe the differences in cost and retail price when price is calculated with and without cash discounts:

16. In cell **H9**, calculate the cost price with the IMU in cell **C14** (Figure 8.4d).

17. In cell **H11**, calculate the retail price with the IMU in cell **C14** (Figure 8.4d).

	A	B	C	D	E	F	G	H
1	*Calculate Initial Markup Percent*							
2	*IMU =*	*Expenses + Profit + Reductions*						
3		*Net Sales + Reductions*						
4								
5	*IMU =*	*Expenses + Profit + Reductions +Alterations - Cash discount*						
6		*Net Sales + Reductions*						
7								
8	Profit	7.0%	Shortage	1.5%		Retail Price	$18.00	
9	Expenses	55.0%	Alterations	3.0%		*Cost Price*	?	
10	Sales Discount	3.0%	Cash Discounts	5.0%				
11	Markdowns	15.0%				*Retail Price*	?	
12						Cost Price	$6.39	
13								
14	*With Cash Discounts*	**IMU**	?					
15	*Without Cash Discounts*	**IMU**	?					

Figure 8.4a Formulas for calculating an IMU with and without cash discounts

	A	B	C	D	E	F	G	H
8	Profit	7.0%	Shortage	1.5%		Retail Price	$18.00	
9	Expenses	55.0%	Alterations	3.0%		*Cost Price*	=G8*(100-C15)	
10	Sales Discount	3.0%	Cash Discounts	5.0%				
11	Markdowns	15.0%				*Retail Price*	=G12/(100-C15)	
12						Cost Price	$6.39	
13								
14	*With Cash Discounts*	**IMU**	=(B8+B9+B10+B11+D8+D9-D10)/(1+B10+B11+D8)					
15	*Without Cash Discounts*	**IMU**	=(B8+B9+B10+B11+D8+D9)/(1+B10+B11+D8)					

Figure 8.4b Formulas for calculating an IMU with and without cash discounts

	A	B	C	D	E	F	G
8	Profit	7.0%	Shortage	1.5%		Retail Price	$18.00
9	Expenses	55.0%	Alterations	3.0%		*Cost Price*	**$5.27**
10	Sales Discount	3.0%	Cash Discounts	5.0%			
11	Markdowns	15.0%				*Retail Price*	**$21.82**
12						Cost Price	$6.39
13							
14	*With Cash Discounts*	**IMU 66.5%**					
15	*Without Cash Discounts*	**IMU 70.7%**					

Figure 8.4c Formulas for calculating an IMU with and without cash discounts

	A	B	C	D	E	F	G	H
8	Profit	7.0%	Shortage	1.5%		Retail Price	$18.00	
9	Expenses	55.0%	Alterations	3.0%		*Cost Price*	**$5.27**	*$6.03*
10	Sales Discount	3.0%	Cash Discounts	5.0%				
11	Markdowns	15.0%				*Retail Price*	**$21.82**	*$19.09*
12						Cost Price	$6.39	
13								
14	*With Cash Discounts*	**IMU 66.5%**						
15	*Without Cash Discounts*	**IMU 70.7%**						

Figure 8.4d Formulas for calculating an IMU with and without cash discounts

How the Maintained Markup Is Used in Planning

Maintained markup is important because it must be large enough to cover operating expenses and profit. Unlike the IMU, a maintained markup is calculated at the *end* of a season from sales and inventory records. However, prior to the season, an estimated maintained markup can be calculated using the planned initial markup and planned reductions to provide an approximation of profitability. Because reductions are planned at retail prices, they must be converted to cost values using the cost complement of the initial markup, as illustrated in the following formula for maintained markups:

Maintained Markup = IMU% – Retail Reductions % * (100% – IMU %)

Application Exercise 8.5 Calculate a Maintained Markup Percent

In this exercise you will calculate a maintained markup percent.

1. Open your *Application Exercises* file.

2. Insert a blank worksheet and type and format the values and labels as shown in Figure 8.5a.

3. Format cell **E7** as **percent, decimal place 1**.

4. Format cells **E8** as **currency, decimal place 0**.

5. Enter the formula in cell **E7** to calculate a maintained markup percent (Figure 8.5b).

6. Enter the formula in cell **E8** to calculate maintained markup dollars (Figures 8.5b and 8.5c).

7. Rename the sheet *Maintained Markup*.

8. Save your file.

Observe the impact of reductions on a maintained markup:

9. Change the markdown percent to *20* and note the decrease in the maintained markup.

10. Click *undo* to reverse the change.

11. Change the markdown, employee discounts, and shortage percents to *zero*.

    Note that the maintained percent is the same as the initial markup.

12. Click *undo* to reverse the change.

Figure 8.5a
Formulas for calculating maintained markup percent and dollar values

	A	B	C	D	E	F
1	*Calculate Maintained Markup Percent*					
2	*MMU % = IMU % – Retail Reductions % * (100% – IMU%)*					
3	*MMU $ = MMU % * Net Sales*					
4						
5	*Calculate Maintained Markup Dollars and Percent*					
6						
7	IMU	63.3%		MMU %	?	
8	Markdown	19.0%		MMU $	?	
9	Employee Discount	3.3%				
10	Shrinkage	2.5%				
11	Planned Net Sales	$328,876				

Figure 8.5b

Formulas for
calculating
maintained markup
percent and dollar
values

	A	B	C	D	E	F
5	*Calculate Maintained Markup Dollars and Percent*					
6						
7	IMU	63.3%		**MMU %**	=B7-(B8+B9+B10)*(1-B7)	
8	Markdown	19.0%		**MMU $**	=E7*B11	
9	Employee Discount	3.3%				
10	Shrinkage	2.5%				
11	Planned Net Sales	$328,876				

Figure 8.5c

Formulas for
calculating
maintained markup
percent and dollar
values

	A	B	C	D	E	F
5	*Calculate Maintained Markup Dollars and Percent*					
6						
7	IMU	63.3%		**MMU %**	54.2%	
8	Markdown	19.0%		**MMU $**	$178,253	
9	Employee Discount	3.3%				
10	Shrinkage	2.5%				
11	Planned Net Sales	$328,876				

When there is a desired maintained markup percent, the maximum allowable percent for reductions can be planned with the following formula:

$$\text{Reductions} = \frac{(\text{IMU\%} - \text{Maintained Markup \%})}{(100\% - \text{Initial Markup \%})}$$

In this formula, the difference between the initial markup and the maintained markup is the *cost* of the reductions. The reductions cost value is converted to its *retail equivalent* with the complement of the initial markup.

Application Exercise 8.6 **Calculate an Allowable Reductions Percent**

In this exercise you will calculate the maximum allowable reductions using the initial markup and a desired maintained markup percent.

1. Open your *Application Exercises* file.

2. Insert a blank worksheet and type and format the values and labels as shown in Figure 8.6a.

3. Format cells **E8** as **percent, decimal place 1**.

4. Format cells **D9** as **currency, decimal place 0**.

5. Enter the formula in cell **E8** to calculate an allowable reductions percent (Figure 8.6b).

6. Enter the formula in cell **E9** to calculate reductions dollars (Figures 8.6b and 8.6c).

7. Rename the sheet *Allowable Reductions*.

8. Save your file.

Observe the impacts of IMUs and maintained markups on reductions:

9. In cell **B9**, change the maintained markup to **53%** and note the increase in allowable reductions.

10. Click *undo* to reverse the change.

11. Decrease the IMU to **60%** and note the decrease in allowable reductions.

12. Click *undo* to reverse the change.

Figure 8.6a
Formula for using a
maintained markup
to calculate an
allowable reductions
percent

	A	B	C	D	E	F
1	*Calculate Allowable Reductions Percent*					
2	*Reductions % = IMU % – MMU % * (100% – IMU %)*					
3	*Reductions $ = Reductions % * Planned Sales*					
4						
5	*Calculate the Maximum Allowable Reductions Percent and Dollar Values*					
6						
7						
8	IMU	63.2%		**Reductions %**	?	
9	Desired MMU	58.0%		**Reductions $**	?	
10	Planned Net Sales	$219,876				

Figure 8.6b
Formula for using a
maintained markup
to calculate an
allowable reductions
percent

	A	B	C	D	E	F
5	*Calculate the Maximum Allowable Reductions Percent and Dollar Values*					
6						
7						
8	IMU	63.2%		**Reductions %**	=(B8-B9)/(1-B8)	
9	Desired MMU	58.0%		**Reductions $**	=E8*B10	
10	Planned Net Sales	$219,876				

Figure 8.6c
Formula for using a
maintained markup
to calculate an
allowable reductions
percent

	A	B	C	D	E	F
5	*Calculate the Maximum Allowable Reductions Percent and Dollar Values*					
6						
7						
8	IMU	63.2%		Reductions %	14.2%	
9	Desired MMU	58.0%		Reductions $	$31,121	
10	Planned Net Sales	$219,876				

Cumulative Markup (CUMU)

A **cumulative markup** is the total markup achieved on an entire department or inventory group over a specific time period. Unlike an initial markup, a cumulative markup is calculated at the *end* of a season after selling has occurred.

The calculation of a cumulative markup requires the detailed accounting of **opening inventory**, **purchases**, **returns**, **freight** costs, markups, and **net transfers**, all of which impact the value of inventory. As shown in Figure 8.7, these factors do not have the same impact on the total cost and retail values. Some have positive effects and increase inventory value, while others have negative effects and decrease value. For example, a freight cost increases while quantity discounts decrease the cost of inventory, but neither impacts retail value. On the other hand, a markup increases the retail value of inventory, but has no impact on the cost value.

A freight cost is calculated as a percent of the purchase cost, as shown in the following formula:

Freight = Freight Percent * Purchases @ Cost

All or a portion of freight costs is charged to the retailer.

Figure 8.7 Factors that impact total cost and retail values

	A	B	C	D	E
2		Cost $	Retail $	Markup %	Cost %
3	Beginning Inventory	$111,665	$286,854		
4	Purchases	$27,102	$86,630		
5	Returns to Vendors	($3,000)	($6,000)		
6	Freight	$798			
7	Quantity Discounts	($800)			
8	Net Transfers	$4,000	$6,000		
9	Net Markup		$5,000		
10	**Total Merchandise Handled/CuMu%**	**$139,765**	**$378,484**	**63.1%**	36.9%
11				↑	
12				CuMu%	

A cumulative markup is the difference between the total retail value and the total cost value of inventory. During a season, because inventory is handled with different costs and retail prices, the cumulative markup reflects an aggregate markup.

Figure 8.7 is an example of a cumulative markup using cost and retail values.

Application Exercise 8.7 Calculate a Cumulative Markup Percent

In this exercise you will calculate a cumulative markup percent.

1. Open your *Application Exercises* file.

2. Insert a blank worksheet and type and format the values and labels as shown in Figure 8.8a.

3. Format cells **B13** and **C13** as **currency, decimal place 0**.

4. Format cells **D13** and **E13** as **percent, decimal place 1**.

5. Enter the formula in cell **B13** to sum cost values (Figure 8.8b).

6. Copy the formula to cell **C13** (Figure 8.8b).

7. Enter the formula in cell **D13** to calculate a cumulative markup percent (Figure 8.8b).

8. Enter the formula in cell **E13** to calculate the cost complement of the cumulative markup (Figure 8.8b).

9. Rename the sheet *CuMu Percent*.

10. Save your file.

Observe the impact on the cumulative markup when the cost and retail values are changed:

11. In cell **C7**, change the opening inventory retail value to **$168,854** and note the decrease in the cumulative markup percent in cell **D13**.

12. Click *undo* to reverse the change.

13. In cell **B8**, change the cost value of purchases to *$29,902* and note the increase in the cumulative markup percent.

14. Click *undo* to reverse the change.

15. In cell **C9**, change the additional markup to *$15,000* and note the increase in the cumulative markup.

16. Click *undo* to reverse the change.

Figure 8.8a

Formula for

calculating a

cumulative markup

percent

	A	B	C	D	E
1	*Calculate Cumulative Markup Percent*				
2	CuMu% =	*Total Retail - Total Cost*			
3		*Total Retail*			
4					
5					
6		**Cost $**	**Retail $**	**Markup %**	**Cost %**
7	Opening Inventory	$143,289	$286,854	50.0%	50.0%
8	Purchases	$39,902	$96,630	58.7%	41.3%
9	Additional Markup		$5,000		
10	Transfers In	$5,000	$8,986		
11	Transfers Out	($3,000)	($6,000)		
12	Freight	$798			
13	**Total Merchandise Handled/CuMu %**	?	?	?	?

Figure 8.8b

Formula for

calculating a

cumulative markup

percent

	A	B	C	D	E
6		**Cost $**	**Retail $**	**Markup %**	**Cost %**
7	Opening Inventory	$143,289	$286,854	50.0%	50.0%
8	Purchases	$39,902	$96,630	58.7%	41.3%
9	Additional Markup		$5,000		
10	Transfers In	$5,000	$8,986		
11	Transfers Out	($3,000)	($6,000)		
12	Freight	$798			
13	**Total Merchandise Handled/CuMu %**	=SUM(B7:B12)	=SUM(C7:C12)	=(C13-B13)/C13	=1-D13

Figure 8.8c

Formula for

calculating a

cumulative markup

percent

	A	B	C	D	E
6		**Cost $**	**Retail $**	**Markup %**	**Cost %**
7	Opening Inventory	$143,289	$286,854	50.0%	50.0%
8	Purchases	$39,902	$96,630	58.7%	41.3%
9	Additional Markup		$5,000		
10	Transfers In	$5,000	$8,986		
11	Transfers Out	($3,000)	($6,000)		
12	Freight	$798			
13	**Total Merchandise Handled/CuMu %**	$185,989	$391,470	52.5%	47.5%

How the Cumulative Markup Is Used in Planning

The cumulative markup is used to calculate the cost value of the **end-ing inventory** under the **retail method of inventory valuation**. The retail method is a perpetual book-inventory system that allows for the cost valu-ation of an ending inventory to be determined at any point in time. The premise of the retail method is that the markup on an ending inventory will approximate the average markup achieved on that same inventory during an accounting period. Because the cumulative markup percent represents the average markup on both new and existing inventories, it is used to determine the cost value of the portion of inventory that remains at the end of a season. The cost of the ending inventory is used to calculate the cost of sales from which gross margin, profit, and loss are calculated. These will be covered in Chapters Nine and Ten of this workbook.

Assignment Five

For your fifth assignment, you will apply Excel skills and retail-math formulas to plan an initial markup percent and project a maintained markup. The initial markup will be used to calculate the cost value of the planned purchases.

1. Open your *Merchandise Budget* file.

2. Check your *Purchases Plan* and correct any formula errors.

3. Create a copy of your *Purchases Plan* sheet and rename the copy *IMU*. Position the *IMU* sheet after the *Purchases* sheet.

Plan a season's percents:

4. In cell **C9**, insert *46.4*% for the operating expense.

5. In cell **C10**, insert *8.6*% for the operating profit.

6. In cell **C11**, insert *1.8*% for the alteration/workroom expense.

7. In cell **C12**, insert *5.0*% for earned cash discounts.

8. In cell **C14**, insert *6.0*% for the freight cost.

Plan an IMU:

9. In cell **C5**, use a formula to plan an IMU for the season.
   Note: Use the value in cell **C19** for the sales percent.

Plan a projected maintained markup (MMU):

10. In cell **C15**, use a formula to plan the projected MMU.

Plan a cost value of purchases:

11. In cell **D51**, enter a formula to plan the cost value of retail purchases for FEB. Use absolute references for the IMU and sales percent in cell **C19** so the formula can be copied to the other months.

12. In cell **C51**, enter a formula to total the monthly purchases at cost.

Calculate a freight cost:

13. In cell **D53**, enter a formula to calculate the freight cost for FEB. Remember that freight costs are based on purchases costs. Use an absolute reference for the freight percent so the formula can be copied to the other months.

14. In cell **C53**, enter a formula to total the monthly freight values.

15. Save your file.

9 *Cost Values*

Chapter Objectives

After reading this chapter, you should be able to:

▶ Define the retail method of inventory.

▶ List the primary advantage of the retail method.

▶ Discuss the importance of calculating cost values.

▶ Distinguish between a perpetual book and a periodic inventory.

▶ List the four calculations required to calculate the cost of sales.

▶ Use Excel and structure retail formulas to calculate:

- Total retail deductions
- Closing inventory retail values
- Closing inventory cost values
- Cost of goods sold

KEY TERMS

The **cost of goods sold** is the cost of inventory, including billed costs and transportation costs.

An **inventory control and valuation system** is an accounting method used to control inventory units and dollar investments.

A **periodic count** is an inventory control system that requires inventory on hand to be physically counted.

A **perpetual-book inventory** is an accounting method that provides the value of available inventory at any point in time.

Profitability refers to the retailer's potential to earn a profit.

Retail deductions refer to inventory that has been sold, marked down, discounted, lost or stolen. Retail deductions are subtracted from the retail value of total merchandise handled to arrive at an ending inventory retail value.

The **retail method of inventory valuation** is a perpetual-book inventory system method that uses the retail value of an ending inventory to estimate the inventory's ending cost value.

Inventory cost values are required for determining profit resulting from retail activities. As illustrated in the following formula, the cost of goods sold is required to arrive at the markup from which profit is derived:

$$
\begin{array}{l}
\text{Sales} \\
-\ \text{Cost of Goods Sold} \\
\hline
=\ \text{Maintained Markup} \\
-\ \text{Operating Expenses} \\
\hline
=\ \text{Operating Profit}
\end{array}
$$

Profitability is influenced by retailer's ability to control inventory cost. For most retailers inventory represents both the single largest investment and asset, so knowledge of its value is important. An accounting system is required to calculate inventory cost and retail dollar values in order to prepare financial statements on which profit and tax liability are based.

THE RETAIL METHOD OF INVENTORY (RMI)

The **retail method of inventory (RMI)** is an **inventory control and valuation system** used by the majority of retailers. The RMI is a **perpetual-book inventory system** that allows a retailer to estimate the cost-value of an ending inventory at any time without having to take a physical count. The cost estimate is based on the average or cumulative markup derived from the total retail and total cost values of related inventories, such as those found in a department. The advantage of the RMI is the convenience of using an average markup to estimate the ending cost of an inventory consisting of multiple units and prices without having to calculate the costs of individual items. Merchandise databases developed with computerized sales and inventory systems, point-of-sales terminals, barcode technology, and tracking systems have eliminated the RMI's major challenge of keeping detailed records of retail price changes, purchase transactions, and the movement of inventory. In the RMI system, the ending-inventory cost is required to determine the costs of goods sold and profit.

Calculations Required for the Retail Method of Inventory Valuation

Under the RMI, several sequential calculations are required prior to calculating the **cost of goods sold**. They include the calculation of:

▶ Total merchandise handled

▶ Cumulative markup and its cost complement

▶ Total retail deductions from an inventory

▶ Ending inventory retail and cost values

Afterward, the cost of goods sold is determined with the following formula:

Total Merchandise Handled at Cost
– Ending Inventory Cost
= Cost of Goods Sold

Total Merchandise Handled

Determining cost and retail values for the total merchandise handled is the starting point for using the retail method of inventory. As illustrated in Chapter Eight, retail and cost values for purchases, inventory returns, net markups, net transfers, and freight are required to calculate the total merchandise handled and the cumulative markup. In addition, accurate cost and retail values must be available for the opening inventory. The opening inventory is the inventory that ended the previous accounting period and under the RMI, its retail and cost values are validated. Prior to recording an opening book inventory, a **periodic count** of inventory is carried out to establish valid cost and retail values.

Cumulative Markup and Cost Complement

The calculation of a cumulative markup was introduced in Chapter Eight in the discussion of markups. Under the RMI, a cumulative markup is required to determine the markup achieved during an accounting period. The cumulative markup percent is based on the total merchandise handled at cost and at retail. The cost complement of the cumulative markup is used to convert the ending inventory retail value to an ending inventory cost value.

Total Retail Deductions

Retail deductions include reductions in the form of markdowns, sales discounts, shortages, and *net sales.* These are totaled to determine the retail value of the inventory deducted from the total merchandise handled. The formula for retail deductions is as follows:

> Net Sales
> + Markdowns
> + Sales Discounts
> + Shortage
> = Total Retail Deductions

Ending Inventory Retail and Cost Values

Ending inventory retail and cost values are determined as follows:

> Total Merchandise Handled Retail Value
> − Total Retail Deductions
> = Ending Inventory Retail Value

> Ending Inventory Cost = Ending Inventory Retail * (100 − Cumulative Markup)

Because an ending inventory cost is calculated with the cost complement of a cumulative or average markup, it represents a reliable *estimate* that can be used to calculate the cost of goods sold as follows:

> Total Merchandise Handled Cost Value
> − Ending Inventory Cost
> = Cost of Goods Sold

As previously explained, the cost of goods sold is required to calculate profitability, which is covered in Chapter Ten.

Application Exercise 9.1 Calculate the Cost of Sales

In Chapter Three, the key elements of a profit-and-loss statement were discussed, and in Chapter Eight, the calculation of a cumulative markup was covered. In this exercise you will use the additional formulas covered in this chapter to begin the development of a profit-and-loss statement. Go back and review the formula for a cumulative markup in Chapter Eight.

1. Open your *Application Exercises* file.

2. Insert a blank worksheet and type and format the values and labels as shown in Figure 9.1a. You will enter formulas in the shaded cells.

3. In cells **D8** and **D9**, enter formulas to calculate the markup percent (Figure 9.1b).

4. In cells **B11** and **C11**, enter formulas to calculate the total cost and retail values of merchandise handled (Figure 9.1b).

5. In cell **F11**, enter the formula to calculate the cumulative markup percent (Figure 9.1b).

6. In cell **C17**, enter the formula to calculate total retail deductions (Figure 9.1b).

7. In cell **C19**, enter the formula to calculate the ending inventory retail value (Figure 9.1b).

8. In cell **B19**, enter the formula to calculate the ending inventory cost value (Figure 9.1b).

9. In cell **B21**, enter the formula to calculate the cost of goods sold (Figures 9.1b and 9.1c).

10. Rename the sheet *Cost of Goods Sold*.

11. Save your file.

Observe how the cost of goods sold is impacted when some of the cost and retail values are increased and decreased:

12. In cell **B8** change the beginning inventory *cost* to *$100,000* and notice that the cumulative markup is increased; total goods handled cost, ending inventory cost, and cost of goods sold are decreased. The retail values are not affected.

13. Click *undo* to reverse the change.

14. In cell **C8** change the beginning inventory *retail* to *$386,854* and notice increases in cumulative markup, total goods handled retail value, and ending inventory retail and cost values. The cost of goods sold is decreased.

15. Click *undo* to reverse the change.

16. In cell **C13** change the retail sales to *$200,000*. Notice increases in cumulative markup, total goods handled retail value, and ending inventory retail and cost values. The cost of goods sold is decreased.

17. Click *undo* to reverse the change.

Figure 9.1a

	A	B	C	D	E	F
1	*Calculate Cost of Goods Sold*					
2	*Total Retail Deductions = Sum of Sales and Retail Reductions*					
3	*Ending Inventory Retail = Total Goods Handled Retail - Total Retail Deductions*					
4	*Ending Inventory Cost = Total Goods Handled Retail * (1- Cumulative Markup%)*					
5	*Cost of Goods Sold = Total Goods Handled Cost - Ending Inventory Cost*					
6						
7		Cost $	Retail $	Markup %	% of Sales	Cumulative Markup
8	Beginning inventory	$121,665	$286,854	?		
9	Purchases	$39,902	$86,630	?		
10	Freight	$5,000				
11	Total Merchandise Handled/CuMu%	?	?			?
12						
13	Sales		$100,000			
14	Markdowns		$15,000			
15	Sales Discounts		$5,000			
16	Shrinkage		$1,000			
17	Total Retail Deductions		?			
18						
19	Ending Inventory	?	?			
20						
21	Cost of Goods Sold	?				

Figure 9.1a Formulas used to calculate the cost of goods sold

Figure 9.1b

	A	B	C	D	E	F
7		Cost $	Retail $	Markup %	% of Sales	Cumulative Markup
8	Beginning inventory	$121,665	$286,854	=(C8-B8)/C8		
9	Purchases	$39,902	$86,630	=(C9-B9)/C9		
10	Freight	$5,000				
11	Total Merchandise Handled	=SUM(B8:B10)	=SUM(C8:C10)			=(C11-B11)/C11
12						
13	Sales		$100,000			
14	Markdowns		$15,000			
15	Sales Discounts		$5,000			
16	Shrinkage		$1,000			
17	Total Retail Deductions		=SUM(C13:C16)			
18						
19	Ending Inventory	=C19*(1-F11)	=C11-C17			
20						
21	Cost of Goods Sold	=B11-B19				

Figure 9.1b Formulas used to calculate the cost of goods sold

	A	B	C	D	E	F
7		Cost $	Retail $	Markup %	% of Sales	Cumulative Markup
8	Beginning inventory	$121,665	$286,854	57.6%		
9	Purchases	$39,902	$86,630	53.9%		
10	Freight	$5,000				
11	Total Merchandise Handled/CuMu%	$166,567	$373,484			55.4%
12						
13	Sales		$100,000			
14	Markdowns		$15,000			
15	Sales Discounts		$5,000			
16	Shrinkage		$1,000			
17	Total Retail Deductions		$121,000			
18						
19	Ending Inventory	$112,603	$252,484			
20						
21	Cost of Goods Sold	$53,964				

Figure 9.1c Formulas used to calculate the cost of goods sold

Assignment Six

For your sixth assignment, you will apply Excel skills and retail-math formulas to plan the total-goods-handled cost value, the cumulative markup percent, and the remaining cost values on your form.

1.   Open your *Merchandise Budget* file.

2.   Check your purchases plan and correct any formula errors.

3.   Create a copy of your *IMU* sheet and rename the copy *Cost Values*.

Position the *Cost Values* sheet after the *IMU* sheet.

4.   In cell **C55**, insert *$40,000* for the Season/Total BOM (opening) inventory cost.

Note that you are being provided with this value because under the RMI, *opening inventory* is merchandise that remains as the ending inventory from the previous accounting period and is not calculated with a formula.

Calculate the opening inventory value for FEB:

5.   In cell **D55**, use the formula to reference the Season/Total BOM (opening inventory) cost.

Note that because FEB begins the season, it naturally assumes the same value as that in cell **C55**.

Plan the total-goods-handled retail value:

6. In cell **D45**, enter the formula to calculate FEB's total-goods-handled retail value. Copy the formula to the other months in cells **E45:I45**.

7. Enter the formula in cell **C45** to calculate the season/total goods handled.

Plan the total-goods-handled cost value for FEB:

8. In cell **D59**, use the formula to calculate the total-goods-handled cost value for FEB. *Do not copy the formula to other months.*

Plan the cumulative markup percent for FEB:

9. In cell **D39**, use the formula to calculate the cumulative markup percent for FEB. *Do not copy the formula to other months.*

Plan the ending inventory cost for FEB:

10. In cell **D57**, use the formula to calculate the ending inventory cost for FEB.

    Note that the ending inventory retail value must be converted to an ending inventory cost using the cost complement of the cumulative markup percent. *It is important that you use an absolute reference for the sales percent in Cell C19 so the formula can be copied to the other months.*

Plan the cost of goods sold for FEB:

11. In cell **D61**, use the formula to calculate the cost of goods sold for FEB.

12. In cell **D55**, use the formula to calculate the BOM for MAR.

    Note that the ending inventory for FEB is the beginning inventory for MAR.

You have completed the calculations for FEB. Because you used cell references, you can simply copy the formula to the other months. Remember that the RMI requires calculations to be in a step sequence. Use the fill handle to copy formulas in the following sequence for MAR:

▶ Total-goods-handled cost

▶ Cumulative markup percent

▶ Ending inventory cost

13. For APR, copy MAR's BOM formula and then start the sequence again until all the months are completed.

14. In cell **C57**, enter the formula to reference JUL's EOM (closing inventory) cost as the season's ending inventory cost.

15. In cell **C59**, enter the formula to calculate the monthly values for total goods handled.

16. In cell **C39**, enter the formula to calculate the season's cumulative markup percent.

17. In cell **C61**, enter the formula to calculate the season/total cost of goods sold value.

18. Save your file.

10 *Gross Margins*

Chapter Objectives

After reading this chapter, you should be able to:

▶ Explain the importance of gross margin.

▶ Distinguish between gross margin and maintained markup.

▶ Explain the difference between the cost of goods and the total cost of goods sold.

▶ Illustrate the impacts of earned cash discounts and alteration expenses on the cost of goods sold.

▶ Illustrate the impacts of earned cash discounts and alteration expenses on a maintained markup.

▶ Use Excel and structure retail formulas to calculate:

- Maintained markup dollars
- Maintained markup percents
- Total costs of goods sold
- Gross-margin dollars
- Gross-margin percents

Gross cost of goods sold is the billed cost of inventory adjusted by trade discounts. Gross cost includes freight cost.

A **gross margin (GM)** refers to net sales, minus the total cost of goods sold. GM is profit from the sale of inventory before operating expenses have been deducted.

A **gross-margin return on an inventory investment (GMROI)** is the ratio that measures the profit generated from the amount of money invested in the inventory. A GMROI is used to direct merchandising and buying decisions.

The **total cost of goods sold** refers to the cost of goods plus the alteration expenses, minus earned cash discounts.

The maintained markup is the difference between net sales and the *cost of goods sold*. The gross margin is the difference between net sales and the **total cost of goods sold**. The **gross cost of goods sold** includes freight and is the billed cost of inventory adjusted by trade discounts.

Credits, in the form of cash discounts are earned by retailers for paying bills prior to their due dates. Cash discounts are important because they are deducted from the billed purchase cost, thereby reducing the cost of goods. Total cost of goods sold takes into consideration cost adjustments in the form of additional expense related to the sale of inventory including alteration and workroom expenses. Alteration or workroom expenses are different from operating expenses because they are related to labor and supplies associated with preparing inventory for sale. These expenses increase the cost of goods sold. As illustrated in the formula below, only in the absence of alteration expense and cash discounts are the maintained markup and gross margin the same.

Net sales	100%
– Cost of goods sold	50%
= **Maintained markup**	**50%**
+ Earned cash discounts	0%
– Alteration expenses	0%
= **Gross margin**	**50%**
– Operating expenses	43%
= Operating profit	7%

Negotiations for cash discounts from vendors are very important to retailers and can make the difference between profit and loss. As illustrated in the two examples below, when there are earned cash discounts, gross margin is increased because discounts reduce the cost of goods sold.

Net Sales	100%		Net Sales	100%
Cost of Goods Sold	50%		Cost of Goods Sold	50%
Cash Discounts	*0%*		*Cash Discounts*	*−5%*
Alteration Expense	3%		Alteration Expense	3%
Total Cost of Goods Sold	53%		Total Cost of Goods Sold	48%
Gross Margin	**47%**		**Gross Margin**	**52%**

CALCULATING GROSS MARGIN (GM)

There are two ways that a gross margin can be viewed:

▶ As the difference between net sales and the total cost of goods

▶ As a factor of a maintained markup, alteration expenses, and earned cash discounts

Calculating GM as the Difference Between Net Sales and the Total Cost of Goods Sold

Chapter Nine covered how to calculate the cost of goods sold using the retail method of inventory (RMI). With the RMI, a gross margin is calculated as follows:

GM = Net Sales – Cost of Goods Sold – Earned Cash Discounts + Alteration Expense

In planning the initial markup, estimates are made for alteration expenses and earned cash discounts based on historical data. However, at the end of a season, when sales have concluded and a gross margin is calculated, the actual dollar values for cash discounts and alteration expenses are available. When earned cash discounts and alteration expenses are stated in percents, they can be converted to dollar values. Alteration expenses are calculated as a percent of sales, and earned cash discounts are calculated on the purchase cost of inventory. Both are expressed on a profit-and-loss statement as a percentage of net sales.

GM dollars are calculated using the dollar values for sales, the cost of goods sold, earned cash discounts, and alteration expenses—all of which provide the *total* cost associated with sales.

Calculating GM as the Maintained Markup Minus Alteration Expenses Plus Earned Cash Discounts

As previously explained, in the absence of cash discounts and alterations, the maintained markup and GM are the same. Therefore, a GM can be calculated by adding the cash discounts and deducting alteration expenses from the maintained markup, as illustrated in the following formula:

GM = Maintained Markup + Earned Cash Discounts − Alteration Expense

As illustrated in the examples below, alteration expenses and earned cash discounts have opposite effects on the maintained markup and cost of goods sold. Alteration expenses increase the cost of goods and decrease the maintained markup. Earned cash discounts decrease the cost of goods sold and increase the maintained markup.

Total Cost of Goods Sold =
Cost of Goods Sold − Earned Cash Discounts + Alteration Expense

GM = Maintained Markup + Earned Cash Discounts − Alteration Expense

Application Exercise 10.1 Calculate Gross-Margin Dollars and Percents

In this exercise you will use your *Cost of Goods Sold* worksheet and continue using the retail method of inventory to calculate the maintained markup and gross-margin dollars and percents.

1. Open your *Application Exercises* file.

2. Make a copy of your completed *Cost of Goods Sold* worksheet.

3. Rename the copy *Gross Margin*.

4. Add the new labels in cells **A23**, **A25**, **A27**, **A29**, **A31**, and **A33** (Figure 10.1a).

5. Format cells **B25**, **B27**, **B29**, **B31**, **D23**, and **D33** as **currency**, **decimal place 0**.

6. Format cells, **E23**, **E25**, **E29**, and E33 as **percent, decimal place 1**.

7. In cells **B25** and **B29**, type the values for alteration expenses and earned cash discounts (Figure 10.1a).

8. In cell **D23**, enter the formula to calculate maintained markup dollars. In cell **E23**, enter the formula to calculate the maintained markup percent of sales (Figure 10.1b).

9. In cell **E25**, enter the formula to calculate the alteration expense percent of sales. In cell **E29**, enter the formula to calculate earned cash discounts as a percent of sales (Figure 10.1b).

	A	B	C	D	E	F
1	*Calculate Maintained Markup and Gross Margin*					
2	*Maintained Markup = Net Sales - Cost of Goods Sold*					
3	*Gross Margin = Net Sales - Total Cost of Goods Sold*					
4	*Gross Cost of Goods Sold = Cost of Goods Sold - Earned Cash Discounts*					
5	*Total Cost of Goods Sold = Gross Cost of Goods Sold + Alteration Expense*					
6						
7		**Cost $**	**Retail $**	**Markup %**	**% of Sales**	**CuMu%**
8	Beginning inventory	$121,665	$286,854	57.6%		
9	Purchases	$39,902	$86,630	53.9%		
10	Freight	$5,000				
11	**Total Merchandise Handled**	**$166,567**	**$373,484**			**55.4%**
12						
13	Sales		$100,000			
14	Markdowns		$15,000			
15	Sales Discounts		$5,000			
16	Shrinkage		$1,000			
17	**Total Retail Deductions**		**$121,000**			
18						
19	**Ending Inventory**	**$112,603**	**$252,484**			
20						
21	**Cost of Goods Sold**	**$53,964**				
22						
23	**Maintained Markup**			?	?	
24						
25	**Earned Cash Discounts**	**($5,793)**			?	
26						
27	**Gross Cost of Goods Sold**	**?**				
28						
29	**Alteration Expense**	**$1,110**				
30						
31	**Total Cost of Goods Sold**	**?**				
32						
33	**Gross Margin**			?	?	

Figure 10.1a Formulas for calculating a maintained markup and a gross margin

Figure 10.1b

Formulas for calculating a maintained markup and a gross margin

	A	B	C	D	E	F
1	*Calculate Maintained Markup and Gross Margin*					
2	*Maintained Markup = Net Sales - Cost of Goods Sold*					
3	*Gross Margin = Net Sales - Total Cost of Goods Sold*					
4	*Gross Cost of Goods Sold = Cost of Goods Sold - Earned Cash Discounts*					
5	*Total Cost of Goods Sold = Gross Cost of Goods Sold + Alteration Expense*					
6						
7		Cost $	Retail $	Markup %	% of Sales	CuMu%
8	Beginning inventory	$121,665	$286,854	57.6%		
9	Purchases	$39,902	$86,630	53.9%		
10	Freight	$5,000				
11	Total Merchandise Handled	$166,567	$373,484			55.4%
12						
13	Sales		$100,000			
14	Markdowns		$15,000			
15	Sales Discounts		$5,000			
16	Shrinkage		$1,000			
17	Total Retail Deductions		$121,000			
18						
19	Ending Inventory	$112,603	$252,484			
20						
21	Cost of Goods Sold	$53,964				
22						
23	Maintained Markup			=C13-B21	=D23/C13	
24						
25	Earned Cash Discounts	($5,793)			=-B25/C13	
26						
27	Gross Cost of Goods Sold	$48,171				
28						
29	Alteration Expense	$1,110				
30						
31	Total Cost of Goods Sold	=SUM(B27,B29)				
32						
33	Gross Margin			=C13-B31	=D33/C13	

Note that because the dollar value for cash discount is a negative number because they are deducted from the cost of goods sold, the formula expressing it as a percent of sales contains a minus sign.

10. In cell **B27**, enter the formula to calculate the gross cost of goods. In cell **B31**, enter the formula to calculate the total cost of goods (Figure 10.1b).

11. In cell **D33**, enter the formula to calculate the gross margin. In cell **E33**, enter the formula to calculate the gross margin as a percent of sales (Figures 10.1b and 10.1c).

12. Save your file.

	A	B	C	D	E	F
1	*Calculate Maintained Markup and Gross Margin*					
2	*Maintained Markup = Net Sales - Cost of Goods Sold*					
3	*Gross Margin = Net Sales - Total Cost of Goods Sold*					
4	*Gross Cost of Goods Sold = Cost of Goods Sold - Earned Cash Discounts*					
5	*Total Cost of Goods Sold = Gross Cost of Goods Sold + Alteration Expense*					
6						
7		**Cost $**	**Retail $**	**Markup %**	**% of Sales**	**CuMu%**
8	Beginning inventory	$121,665	$286,854	57.6%		
9	Purchases	$39,902	$86,630	53.9%		
10	Freight	$5,000				
11	**Total Merchandise Handled**	**$166,567**	**$373,484**			**55.4%**
12						
13	Sales		$100,000			
14	Markdowns		$15,000			
15	Sales Discounts		$5,000			
16	Shrinkage		$1,000			
17	**Total Retail Deductions**		**$121,000**			
18						
19	**Ending Inventory**	**$112,603**	**$252,484**			
20						
21	**Cost of Goods Sold**	**$53,964**				
22						
23	**Maintained Markup**			**$46,036**	**46.0%**	
24						
25	**Earned Cash Discounts**	**($5,793)**			**5.8%**	
26						
27	**Gross Cost of Goods Sold**	**$48,171**				
28						
29	**Alteration Expense**	**$1,110**			**1.1%**	
30						
31	**Total Cost of Goods Sold**	**$49,281**				
32						
33	**Gross Margin**			**$50,719**	**50.7%**	

Examine the impacts of alteration expenses and earned cash discounts on the cost of goods sold and the maintained markup:

13. In cell **B21**, notice that the cost of goods sold is $53,964. Alteration expense dollars in cell **B25** increased the cost to $55,074, but earned-cash-discount dollars in cell **B29** offset the increase, which resulted in a total-cost-of-goods-sold value of $49,281 (Figure 10.1c).

14. In cell **E23**, notice that the maintained markup percent is 46.0%. The alteration percent of 1.1% in cell **E25** decreased the markup, but the earned cash discount percent of 5.8% offset the decrease and resulted in a higher gross margin (Figure 10.1c).

15. In cell **B25**, reduce the alteration expense to *$0.00* and observe the impact of a decreased gross cost-of-goods-sold value and an increased GM. Click *undo* to reverse the change.

16. In cell **B29**, reduce the earned cash discounts to *$0.00* and observe the impact of an increased total-cost-of-goods-sold value and a decreased GM.

17. Click *undo* to reverse the change.

18. In cells **B25** and **B29**, reduce both the alteration expense and earned cash discounts to *$0.00* and notice that the maintained markup and GM have the same values.

19. Click *undo* twice to reverse the changes.

GROSS-MARGIN RETURN ON INVENTORY INVESTMENT (GMROI)

Gross-margin return on inventory investment (GMROI), pronounced *jim-roys*, are measures of productivity and sales efficiency. As a profit measure, a GMROI indicates the number of dollars earned in profit for each dollar invested in inventory. The gross margin is the profit, and the cost of inventory represents the investment. The formula for a GMROI is:

$$\text{GMROI} = \frac{\text{Gross Margin Dollars}}{\text{Average Inventory Cost}}$$

The cost of the average inventory is calculated as follows:

$$\text{Average Inventory Cost} = \text{Average Inventory Retail} * (100 - \text{CuMu \%})$$

The cumulative, or aggregate, markup percent, instead of the initial markup percent, is used to convert the average inventory to a cost value. As explained in Chapter Eight, the average inventory includes the opening inventory from a previous period and the merchandise purchased during a current accounting period; therefore, the cumulative markup provides a more accurate estimate of inventory cost.

A GMROI can also be viewed as a measure of sales efficiency relative to profit, sales, and stockturn. A GMROI answers the question of how many inventory turnovers produced the profit results. This measure requires the following formula:

$$\text{GMROI} = \frac{\text{Gross Margin \%} * \text{Stockturn}}{(100 - \text{CuMu \%})}$$

Calculating a GMROI as a profit ratio or as a measure of sales efficiency will produce the same results, which can be expressed in dollars or as the percentage of returns.

EVALUATING ACCEPTABLE GMROIs

For the most meaningful result—one that will allow a retailer to respond—a GMROI should be calculated for a department, product line, SKU, or vendor. For example, merchandise that provides the lowest rate of return can be dropped, or measures could be developed to either improve sales results or lower inventory costs. Interpretation of GMROI results can be evaluated against industry standards for retailers of a similar size, similar merchandise, and/or similar sales volume. Ideally, the specific interpretation of GMROI results should be defined within each retail organization because companies vary in their criteria for acceptability.

A GMROI of $1 or 100 percent represents a return of zero, because for every dollar invested in inventory, one dollar was returned. This rate of return suggests that neither profit nor expenses can be covered. A GMROI of $2 may not provide profit, while a return of $3 or higher is best, and may cover both expenses and profit. However, because GMROI calculations ignore expenses, it is impossible to provide a definitive answer to what is an acceptable return. Given the fact that some merchandise can have high sales and a low gross margin, the primary benefit of GMROI analysis is that it allows retailers to make merchandising decisions based on returns on investments rather than on sales.

Application Exercise 10.2 **Calculate Gross-Margin Return on Inventory Investment**

In this exercise you will calculate a GMROI in dollars and percents. First you will calculate all values required in the GMROI formulas. Then you will use use them to calculate a return on an investment. Afterward, you will develop one complex formula to calculate a GMROI without using the previously calculated values.

1. Open your *Application Exercises* file.

2. Insert a blank worksheet and type and format the values and labels as shown in Figure 10.2a.

3. Format **B15**, **B17**, and **B18** as **currency, decimal place 0**.

4. Format **E8:E9** as **currency, decimal places 2**.

5. Format cell **B16** as **percent, decimal place 1**. Format cells **E11:E12** as **percent, decimal place 0**.

6. Format cell **B19** as **number, decimal place 1**.

7. Enter the formulas to calculate values for cells **B15:B19** (Figure 10.2b).

8. In cell **E8**, enter a formula to calculate GMROI dollars using your pre-calculated values in cells **B15:B19** (Figure 10.2c).

9. In cell **E11**, enter a formula to calculate a GMROI percent using your precalculated values in cells **B15:B19** (Figure 10.2c).

10. Using *only* the values in cells **B8:B12**, try combining all required calculations for GMROI *dollars* to develop one complex formula. Insert that formula in cell **E9** (Figure 10.2c).

    Note: The value should be the same as that in cell **E8**. See Figure 10.2d.

11. Using *only* the values in cells **B8:B12**, try combining all required calculations for a GMROI *percent* to develop one complex formula. Insert that formula in cell **E12** (Figure 10.2c).

    Note: The value should be the same as that in cell **E11**. See Figure 10.2d.

	A	B	C	D	E	F	G
1	*Calculate Gross Margin Return on Inventory Investment (GMROI)*						
2	*GMROI $ = Gross Margin / Average Inventory Cost*						
3	*Average Inventory Cost = Average Inventory Retail * (1- CuMu%)*						
4							
5	*GMROI %= (Gross Margin% * Stockturn) / (1- CuMu%)*						
6	*Stockturn = Sales / Average Inventory*						
7							
8	Sales	$96,000	**GMROI $**		?		
9	Beginning Inventory Retail	$30,345			?	*One complex formula*	
10	Ending Inventory Retail	$25,679					
11	Total Cost of Sales	$49,972	**GMROI %**		?		
12	CuMu %	48.9%			?	*One complex formula*	
13							
14	*Pre Calculations*						
15	Gross Margin Dollars	?					
16	Gross Margin Percent	?					
17	Average Inventory Retail	?					
18	Average Inventory Cost	?					
19	Stockturn	?					

Figure 10.2a Formulas for calculating a gross-margin return on an investment

	A	B	C	D	E	F	G
8	Sales	$96,000		**GMROI $**	?		
9	Beginning Inventory Retail	$30,345			?	*One complex formula*	
10	Ending Inventory Retail	$25,679					
11	Total Cost of Sales	$49,972		**GMROI %**	?		
12	CuMu %	48.9%			?	*One complex formula*	
13							
14	*Pre Calculations*						
15	Gross Margin Dollars	=B8-B11					
16	Gross Margin Percent	=B15/B8					
17	Average Inventory Retail	=AVERAGE(B9:B10)					
18	Average Inventory Cost	=B17*(1-B12)					
19	Stockturn	=B8/AVERAGE(B9:B10)					

Figure 10.2b Formulas for calculating a gross-margin return on an investment

	A	B	C	D	E	F	G	H	I
8	Sales	$96,000		GMROI $	=B15/B18				
9	Beginning Inventory Retail	$30,345			=(B8-B11)/(AVERAGE(B9:B10)*(1-B12))				
10	Ending Inventory Retail	$25,679							
11	Total Cost of Sales	$49,972		GMROI %	=(B16*B19)/(1-B12)				
12	CuMu %	48.9%			=(B8-B11)/B8*(B8/AVERAGE(B9:B10))/(1-B12)				
13									
14	*Pre Calculations*								
15	Gross Margin Dollars	$46,028							
16	Gross Margin Percent	47.9%							
17	Average Inventory Retail	$28,012							
18	Average Inventory Cost	$14,311							
19	Stockturn	3.4							

Figure 10.2c Formulas for calculating a gross-margin return on an investment

Figure 10.2d

Formulas for calculating a gross-margin return on an investment

	A	B	C	D	E
8	Sales	$96,000		**GMROI $**	**$3.22**
9	Beginning Inventory Retail	$30,345			**$3.22**
10	Ending Inventory Retail	$25,679			
11	Total Cost of Sales	$49,972		**GMROI %**	**322%**
12	CuMu %	48.9%			**322%**
13					
14	*Pre Calculations*				
15	Gross Margin Dollars	$46,028			
16	Gross Margin Percent	47.9%			
17	Average Inventory Retail	$28,012			
18	Average Inventory Cost	$14,311			
19	Stockturn	3.4			

Notice that the GMROI represents $3.22 for every $1.00 invested in inventory, and that it represents a return of 322% (Figure 10.2d).

12. Rename the sheet *GMROI*.

13. Save your file.

Observe ways that the GMROI is increased and decreased:

14. In cell **B8**, change the sales value to *$76,000* and note the decrease in the GMROI. Click *undo* to reverse the change.

15. In cell **B10**, change the ending inventory cost to *$19,000* and note the increase in the GMROI. Click *undo* to reverse the change.

16. In cell **B12**, change the cumulative markup percent to *60%* and note the increase in the GMROI. Click *undo* to reverse the change.

Assignment Seven

Assume that the sales and inventory objectives previously planned on your form were achieved. For your seventh assignment you will apply your Excel skills and knowledge of retail math formulas to calculate gross margin, and GMROI.

1. Open your *Merchandise Budget* file.

2. Check your cost values and correct any formula errors.

3. Create a copy of your *Cost Values* sheet. Rename the copy *Gross Margin*. Position the *gross margin* sheet after the *cost values* sheet.

4. Enter the formula in cell **C47** to calculate season/total gross margin dollars. Use absolute references for earned cash discounts and alteration expense so formula can be copied to other cells.

5. Enter the formula in cell **C48** to calculate season/total gross margin percent.

6. Copy the gross margin-dollar and percent formulas to the six months.

7. In cell **C16**, enter the formula to calculate GMROI dollars for the season.

8. Save your file.

Assignment Eight

Your planning form is completed. Assuming that all goes as you have planned your final assignment requires you to use your knowledge of Excel and the retail method of inventory to develop profit/loss statements to evaluate profitability.

To complete this assignment you will need your:

▶ *Merchandise Budget file*

▶ *Application Exercises file*

So that you will not have to develop another GM form, you will copy the one from your *Application Exercises* file to your *Merchandise Budget* file.

1. Open *both* files.

2. From your *Application Exercises* file click on your *Gross Margin* sheet tab.

3. Select and *copy* the range **A7:F33**, which includes the values and labels on the GM form. See Figure 10.3.

4. On the *Gross Margin* sheet in your *Merchandise Budget* file, click in cell **K2**. Select *paste special* from the paste tool and then select *values and number formats* to copy the range to your GM sheet. See Figure 10.4. Save your Merchandise *Budget* file but do not close it.

5. Close your *Application Exercises* file.

Format the Profit/Loss Form

6. Expand **column K** to a width of **30**. Expand **columns L–P** to a width of **13**.

7. Delete all the *values* from range **L3:P28.** *Do not* delete the row or column headings.

8. In **K30**, type the label **Operating Expense.** In **K32**, type the label **Operating Profit**.

9. Format cells **N30:N32** as **currency, decimal place 0.** Format cells **O30:O32** as **percent, decimal place 1.** *Center align* these cells.

10. In **Row 1**, Merge and Center" cells **K1:P1.**

11. Select range **K1:P32** and format *font size* as **14.**

12. Insert a formula to reference cell **D17** (FEB) as the title for this profit/loss statement.

13. Save your file.

Reference values from your Planning Form.

14. Figure 10.5 is an example of the form that you are developing. You will use formula in cells to reference from your planning form, cost and retail values required to complete the profit loss report for Feb. See Figure 10.5.

	A	B	C	D	E	F
7		Cost $	Retail $	Markup %	% of Sales	CuMu%
8	Beginning inventory	$121,665	$286,854	57.6%		
9	Purchases	$39,902	$86,630	53.9%		
10	Freight	$5,000				
11	Total Merchandise Handled	$166,567	$373,484			55.4%
12						
13	Sales		$100,000			
14	Markdowns		$15,000			
15	Sales Discounts		$5,000			
16	Shrinkage		$1,000			
17	Total Retail Deductions		$121,000			
18						
19	Ending Inventory	$112,603	$252,484			
20						
21	Cost of Goods Sold	$53,964				
22						
23	Maintained Markup			$46,036	46.0%	
24						
25	Earned Cash Discounts	($5,793)			5.8%	
26						
27	Gross Cost of Goods Sold	$55,074				
28						
29	Alteration Expense	$1,110			1.1%	
30						
31	Total Cost of Goods Sold	$49,281				
32						
33	Gross Margin			$50,719	50.7%	

Figure 10.3 Copy the gross margin form from the application exercises file.

Note that the operating expense should be an absolute reference for this exercise because we are using the season's planned percent to calculate monthly dollar values as a percent of sales.

15. After you have referenced all of the required values from your planning form, enter formulas in the cell labeled with "F" to calculate the required values to arrive at GM and operating profit.

Note if you used the correct formulas, the values on your profit loss statement should match those on your planning form. If they don't,

Figure 10.4 Paste *GM* form next to planning form in cell **K2**.

	H (JUN)	I (JUL)
17	**JUN**	**JUL**
18	$44,100	$43,313
19	16.8%	16.5%
21	$75,300	$74,625
22	1.71	1.72
23	$74,625	$75,000
25	$7,861	$7,952
26	17.83%	18.36%
27	17.3%	17.5%
29	$2,709	$2,630
30	6.1%	6.1%
31	17.2%	16.7%
33	$877	$877
34	2.0%	2.0%
35	16.7%	16.7%
37	$54,872	$55,146
39	59.1%	59.1%
41	$74,963	$74,813
43	0.59	0.58
45	$130,172	$129,771
47	$29,932	$29,460
48	67.9%	68.0%
50	**JUN**	**JUL**
51	$21,156	$21,262
53	$1,269	$1,276
55	$30,770	$30,496
57	$30,496	$30,650
59	$53,195	$53,033
61	$22,699	$22,383

	Cost $	Retail $	Markup %	% of Sales	CuMu%
Beginning	$121,665	$286,854	57.6%		
Purchases	$39,902	$86,630	53.9%		
Freight	$5,000				
Total Mer	$166,567	$373,484			55.4%
Sales		$100,000			
Markdowns		$15,000			
Sales Discounts		$5,000			
Shrinkage		$1,000			
Total Retail Deductic		$121,000			
Ending In	$112,603	$252,484			
Cost of Go	$53,964				
Maintained Markup				$46,036	46.0%
Earned C	($5,793)				5.8%
Gross Cost	$55,074				
Alteration	$1,110				1.1%
Total Cost	$49,281				
Gross Margin				$50,719	50.7%

	J	K	L	M	N	O	P
1			=D17				
2			Cost $	Retail $	Markup %	% of Sales	CuMu%
3		Beginning inventory	=D55	=D21	F		
4		Purchases	=D51	=D37	F		
5		Freight	=D53				
6		**Total Merchandise Handled**	F	F			F
7							
8		Sales		=D18			
9		Markdowns		=D25			
10		Sales Discounts		=D29			
11		Shrinkage		=D33			
12		**Total Retail Deductions**		F			
13							
14		**Ending Inventory**	F	F			
15							
16		**Cost of Goods Sold**	F				
17							
18		**Maintained Markup**			F	F	
19							
20		**Earned Cash Discounts**	F			F	
21							
22		**Gross Cost of Goods Sold**	F				
23							
24		**Alteration Expense**	F			F	
25							
26		**Total Cost of Goods Sold**	F				
27							
28		**Gross Margin**			F	F	
29							
30		**Operating Expense**			F	=$C$9	
31							
32		**Operating Profit**			F	F	

Figure 10.5 Referenced values required for formulas to calculate a GM and an operating profit

check to make sure that you referenced the correct values for FEB and used the correct formulas.

16. Save your file,

Complete profit/loss statements for the remaining months.

Remember that you have used cell references, and all of the values for FEB's profit/loss statement were referenced from **column D** on your planning form. See Figure 10.5. For MAR all of the values will be referenced from column E, for APR values will be referenced from column F etc.

17. Highlight the *columns* **K** through **P** and copy and paste FEB's statement to column **R** to develop MAR statement

18. In cell **S3**, enter the formula =**L14** to reference FEB ending inventory cost as MAR beginning inventory cost. In cell **T3** enter the formula =**M14** to reference FEB ending inventory retail as MAR beginning inventory retail value.

19. From the formula bar, replace only the *column* reference "*D*" in cells **R1, S4, T3, S5, T4** and **T8:T11** with "E" because all of the required values for MAR are from the same *rows* as FEB. The remainders of the values are calculated with formulas.

    Note that you must replace *seven* column references because the other is an absolute reference and should not be changed. See Figure 10.4. You can replace each column reference manually or you can select *only* the cells that you need to change and use Excel's *Find/Replace* feature in the Editing group on the Home tab.

20. After you complete and check the MAR statement, highlight and copy *columns* **R** through **W** and skip one column over and paste in column **Y** to develop APR. GM form.

    Note that for APR, the beginning inventory cost and retail values are automatically referenced from MAR.

21. Replace the *eight* column references with "**F**" to extract APR values into the profit/loss statement.

22. Save your file and repeat copying the previous month and replacing column references until you complete the remaining three months.

23. Check each month to see that the GM $ and GM % match those on your planning form.

You have completed profit-and-loss statements for six months. Your *Gross Margin* worksheet is interactive. If you change values in any of the cells on your *planning* form that *do not* contain formulas, your profit-and-loss statements will automatically adjust to reflect a new GM and operating profit. At this point you can analyze one of the statements to see how profits were impacted by the values you planned.

Appendix:
Excel Formulas

SALES

$$\text{Average Sales} = \frac{\text{Sales}}{\text{Number of } \textit{Weeks or Months} \text{ in Period}}$$

Net Sales = Gross Sales – Customer Returns and Allowances

$$\text{Percent Change} = \frac{(\text{Current Period} - \text{Prior Period})}{\text{Prior Period}}$$

$$\text{Percent Change} = \left(\frac{\text{Current Period}}{\text{Prior Period}} \right) - 1$$

$$\text{Percent-to-Total} = \frac{\text{Part}}{\text{Total}}$$

Sales *(Decrease)* = Last Season's Sales – (Last Season's Sales * % Decrease)

Sales *(Increase)* = Last Season's Sales + (Last Season's Sales * % Increase)

Sales = Average Inventory * Stockturn

Sales = Number of Units Sold * Average Unit Retail Price

INVENTORY

Average Inventory *(Month)* = Average of Month's BOM and EOM

Average Inventory *(Season)* = Average of Six BOMs and Last Month's EOM

Average Inventory *(Year)* = Average of 12 BOMs and Last Month's EOM

$$\text{Average Inventory} = \frac{\text{Sales}}{\text{Stockturn}}$$

$$\text{Average Unit Retail Price} = \frac{\text{Sales}}{\text{Number of Units Sold}}$$

Basic Stock = Average Season's Inventory – Average Season's Sales

BOM Inventory *(Basic Stock Method)* = Basic Stock + Month's Planned Sales

BOM Inventory *(Percentage Variation Method)* =

$$\text{Season's Average Inventory} * 0.50 \left(\frac{1 + \text{Month's Planned Sales}}{\text{Average Monthly Sales}} \right)$$

BOM Inventory = Previous Month's EOM Inventory

BOM Inventory *(Stock-to-Sales Ratio Method)* =

Stock-to-Sales Ratio * Month's Planned Sales

BOM Inventory *(Weeks-of-Supply Method)* =

Average Weekly Sales * Number of Weeks Supply

Ending Inventory Retail Value =

Total Merchandise Handled Retail Value – Total Retail Deductions

EOM Inventory = BOM Inventory for Following Month

$$\text{Number of Units Sold} = \frac{\text{Sales}}{\text{Average Unit Retail Price}}$$

$$\text{Number of Weeks Supply} = \frac{\text{Number of Weeks in Period}}{\text{Stockturn for Period}}$$

$$\text{Sell-through \%} = \frac{\text{Number of Units Sold}}{(\text{Number of Units on Hand} + \text{Number of Units Sold})}$$

$$\text{Sell-through \%} = \frac{\text{Sales}}{(\$ \text{ Units on Hand} + \text{Sales})}$$

Stock-to-Sales Ratio = BOM Inventory / Month's Sales

$$\text{Stockturn} = \frac{\text{Sales for Period}}{\text{Average Inventory for Same Period}}$$

Total Merchandise Handled at Retail =

Beginning Inventory (*Retail*) + Net Purchases (*Retail*)
+ Net Transfers (*Retail*) + Net Markup

Total Retail Deductions = Net sales + Net Markdowns + Shrinkage + Sales Discounts

REDUCTIONS

Discount % of Sales = $\dfrac{\text{Dollar Discount}}{\text{Net Sales}}$

Discount Price = Retail Price (100% – Sales Discount %)

Dollar Discount = Discount % * Net Sales

Dollar Discount Distributions = Season's Dollar Discount * Discount Distribution %

Dollar Markdown = Markdown % * Net Sales

Dollar Markdown = Original Retail Price – New Retail Price

Dollar Markdown Distributions =

Season's Dollar Markdown * Markdown Distribution %

Dollar Shrinkage = Shrinkage % * Net Sales

Dollar Shrinkage Distributions =

Season's Dollar Shrinkage * Shrinkage Distribution %

Markdown % of Sales = $\dfrac{\text{Dollar Markdown}}{\text{Net Sales}}$

Off-Retail Markdown % = $\dfrac{(\text{Original Retail Price} - \text{New Retail Price})}{\text{Original Retail Price}}$

Reductions = Markdown + Sales Discount + Shrinkage

Retail Reductions % = $\dfrac{(\text{Initial Markup \%} - \text{Maintained Markup \%})}{(100\% - \text{Initial Markup \%})}$

Shortage (Shrinkage) = Closing Book Inventory Retail Value – Physical Inventory

Shrinkage % of Sales = $\dfrac{\text{Dollar Shrinkage}}{\text{Net Sales}}$

Total-Dollar Markdown = (Original Retail Price – New Retail Price) * Number of Units

Total Retail Price = Retail Price * Number of Units

PURCHASES

$$\text{Average Unit Retail Price} = \frac{\text{Sales}}{\text{Number of Units}}$$

Monthly Purchases = Month's Sales + EOM + Month's Reductions – BOM

Purchases = Merchandise Needed – Merchandise Available

Purchases at Cost = Purchases at Retail (100% – Initial Markup %)

$$\text{Purchases at Retail} = \frac{\text{Purchases at Cost}}{(100\% - \text{Initial Markup \%})}$$

OTB for the Balance of a Month Based on EOM = (Planned EOM + Planned Sales for the Balance of a Month + Planned Reductions for the Balance of a Month) – (Inventory on Hand + Month's Inventory on Order)

OTB for the Balance of a Month Based on Purchases = Month's Planned Purchases – (Month's Inventory Received to Date + Month's Inventory on Order)

OTB = (Sales + EOM + Reductions) – (BOM + Month's Inventory on Order)

MARKUP

Cost = Retail – Markup

$$\text{Cumulative Markup \%} = \frac{(\text{Total Merchandise Handled } \textit{Retail} - \text{Total Merchandise Handled } \textit{Cost})}{\text{Total Merchandise Handled } \textit{Retail}}$$

Dollar Markup = Retail Price – Cost Price

$$\text{Initial Markup \%} = \frac{(\text{Maintained Markup + Reductions})}{(\text{Net Sales + Reductions})}$$

$$\text{Initial Markup \%} = \frac{(\text{Expenses + Profit + Markdown + Sales Discount + Shrinkage})}{(\text{Net Sales + Reductions})}$$

$$\text{Initial Markup \%} = \frac{(\text{Expenses + Profit + Reductions + Alterations – Cash Discounts})}{(\text{Net Sales + Reductions})}$$

Maintained Markup = Net Sales – Gross Cost of Merchandise Sold

Maintained Markup % = (Initial Markup % – Retail Reductions %) * (100% – Initial Markup %)

$$\text{Maintained Markup \%} = \frac{\text{Dollar Maintained Markup}}{\text{Net Sales}}$$

Markup = Retail – Cost

$$\text{Markup \% on Cost} = \frac{\text{Dollar Markup}}{\text{Cost Price}}$$

$$\text{Markup \% on Entire Inventory} = \frac{\text{Total Dollar Markup}}{\text{Total Retail Price}}$$

$$\text{Markup \% on Retail} = \frac{\text{Dollar Markup}}{\text{Retail Price}}$$

$$\text{Retail Price} = \frac{\text{Cost Price}}{(100\% - \text{Markup \%})}$$

Retail = Cost + Markup

Total Cost Price = Cost Price * Number of Units

Total Dollar Markup = Total Retail Price – Total Cost Price

COST VALUES

Average Inventory Cost = Average Inventory Retail (100% – Cumulative Markup %)

Cost of Goods Sold = Total Merchandise Handled at Cost – Ending Inventory Cost

$$\text{Cost of Goods Sold \%} = \frac{\text{Dollar Cost of Goods Sold}}{\text{Net Sales}}$$

Cost Price = Retail Price (100% – Markup %)

Dollar Freight = Freight % * Purchases Cost *(Invoice)*

Ending Inventory Cost Value =
Ending Inventory Retail Value (100% – Cumulative Markup %)

$$\text{Freight \%} = \frac{\text{Dollar Freight}}{\text{Purchases Cost } (Invoice)}$$

Total Cost of Goods Sold =
Cost of Goods Sold + Alteration Expense – Earned Cash Discounts

Total Merchandise Handled at Cost = Beginning Inventory *(Cost)* + Net Purchases
(Cost) + Net Transfers *(Cost)* + Freight

PROFIT

Gross Margin = Maintained Markup – Alteration Expense + Earned Cash Discounts

Gross Margin = Sales – Total Cost of Sales

$$\text{Gross Margin \%} = \frac{\text{Dollar Gross Margin}}{\text{Net Sales}}$$

$$\text{Gross Margin Return on Inventory (GMROI)} = \frac{\text{Dollar Gross Margin}}{\text{Average Inventory Cost}}$$

Net Profit or Loss = Operating Profit − Other Expense + Other Income

$$\text{Net Profit or Loss \%} = \frac{\text{Dollar Net Profit}}{\text{Net Sales}}$$

Operating Expense = Operating Expense % * Net Sales

$$\text{Operating Expense \%} = \frac{\text{Dollar Operating Expense}}{\text{Net Sales}}$$

Operating Profit or Loss = Gross Margin − Operating Expense

$$\text{Operating Profit or Loss \%} = \frac{\text{Dollar Operating Profit}}{\text{Net Sales}}$$

Bibliography

Anderson, Carol. 1993. *Retailing: Concepts, strategy and information.* St. Paul, MN: West Publishing.

Berman, Barry, and Joel R. Evans. 2003. *Retail management: A strategic approach*, 9th ed. New York: Pearson Education.

Bohlinger, Maryanne S. 2001. *Merchandise buying*, 5th ed. NewYork: Fairchild Books.

Cash, R. Patrick, Chris Thomas, John W. Wingate, and Joseph S. Friedlander. 2005. *Management of retail buying.* New York: John Wiley & Sons.

Connell, Dana. 2010. *A buyer's life: Planning & forecasting 365.* New York: Fairchild Books.

Diamond, Ellen. 2006. *Fashion retailing: A multi-channel approach.* Upper Saddle River, NJ: Prentice Hall.

Dion, Jim, and Ted Topping. 2002. *Retail business.* Bellingham, WA: Self-Counsel Press.

Donnellan, John. 2007. *Merchandise buying and management*, 3rd ed. New York: Fairchild Books.

Dunne, Patrick M., and Robert F. Lusch. 2005. *Retailing*. Florence, KY: South-Western College Publishing.

Easterling, Cynthia R., Ellen L. Flottman, Marian H. Jernigan, and Beth E. S. Wuest. 2007. *Merchandising mathematics for retailing*, 4th ed. Upper Saddle River, NJ: Prentice Hall.

Kincade, Doris H., Fay Y. Gibson, and Ginger A. Woodard. 2003. *Merchandising math: A managerial approach*. Upper Saddle River, NJ: Prentice Hall.

Levy, Michael, and Barton A. Weitz. 2008. *Retailing management*, 7th ed. New York: McGraw-Hill.

Mazur, Paul. 1927. *Principles of organization applied to modern retailing*. NewYork: Harper & Brothers.

Moore, Evelyn C. 2004. *Math for merchandising: A step-by-step approach*, 3rd ed.Upper Saddle River, NJ: Prentice Hall.

Parham, Susan. 2002. *Math for merchants*. Portland, Oregon: Susan Parham Lessons Learned.

Poloian, Lynda G. 2003. *Retailing principles: A global outlook*, 3rd ed. New York: Fairchild Books.

Rabolt, Nancy J., and Judy K. Miler. 2009. *Concepts and cases in retail and merchandise management*, 2nd ed. New York: Fairchild Books.

Tepper, Bette K. 2008. *Mathematics for retail buying*, 6th ed. New York: Fairchild Books.

Weeks, Andrea L., Veronica Miller Mordaunt, and Dorothy A. Metcalfe. 1991. *Effective marketing management: Using merchandising and financial strategies for retail success*. New York: Fairchild Books.

Index